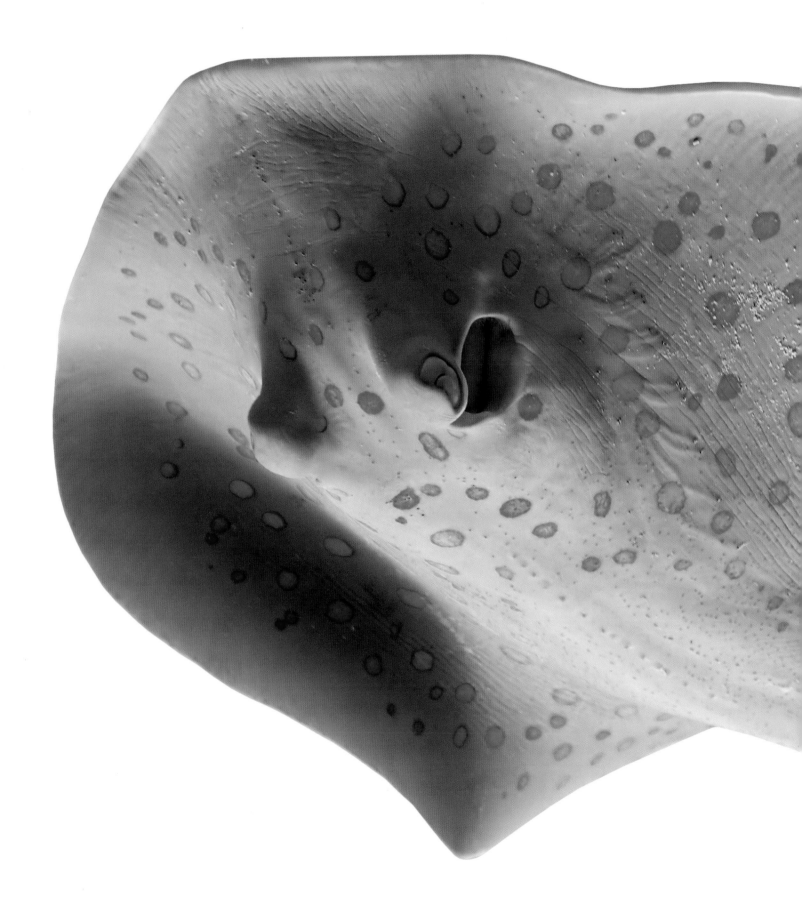

Published by Creative Education and
Creative Paperbacks
P.O. Box 227, Mankato, Minnesota 56002
Creative Education and Creative Paperbacks
are imprints of The Creative Company
www.thecreativecompany.us

Design by The Design Lab
Production by Chelsey Luther
Art direction by Rita Marshall
Printed in the United States of America

Photographs by Alamy (Design Pics Inc., Nature Pic-
ture Library), Dreamstime (Appolloman, Berndneeser,
Digitaldiver, Jiaking1, Worapat Maitriwong, Kiryl
Paddubski), Getty Images (Michael Melford, WIN-
Initiative), iStockphoto (EXTREME-PHOTOGRAPHER) ,
Minden Pictures (Claudio Contreras)

Library of Congress Cataloging-in-Publication Data
Names: Bodden, Valerie.
Title: Rays / Valerie Bodden.
Series: Amazing Animals.
Includes bibliographical references and index.
Summary: A basic exploration of the appearance,
behavior, and habitat of rays, the flat-bodied fish
with skeletons made of cartilage. Also included is
a story from folklore explaining why rays' fins look
like wings.
Identifiers: ISBN 978-1-60818-882-6 (hardcover)
/ ISBN 978-1-62832-498-3 (pbk) / ISBN 978-1-
56660-934-0 (eBook)

This title has been submitted for CIP processing under
LCCN 2017937605.

CCSS: RI.1.1, 2, 4, 5, 6, 7; RI.2.2, 5, 6, 7, 10;
RI.3.1, 5, 7, 8; RF.1.1, 3, 4; RF.2.3, 4

First Edition HC 9 8 7 6 5 4 3 2 1
First Edition PBK 9 8 7 6 5 4 3 2 1

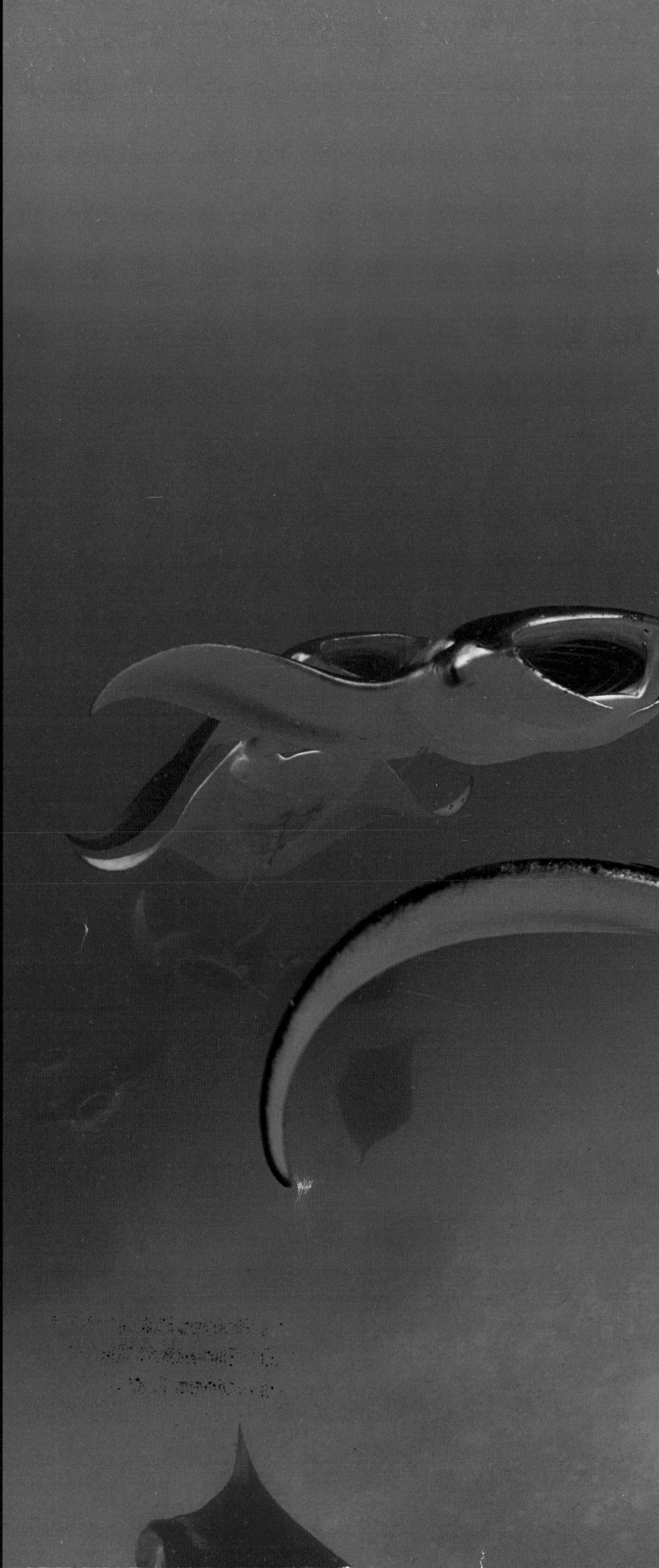

AMAZ*I*NG ANIMALS

RAYS

BY VALERIE BODDEN

CREATIVE EDUCATION · CREATIVE PAPERBACKS

Rays use their long, thin tails to steer through water

Rays are fish related to sharks. More than 160 kinds of rays live in **oceans**. Stingrays, electric rays, and manta rays are kinds of rays. Sawfish are a kind of ray, too.

oceans big areas of deep, salty water

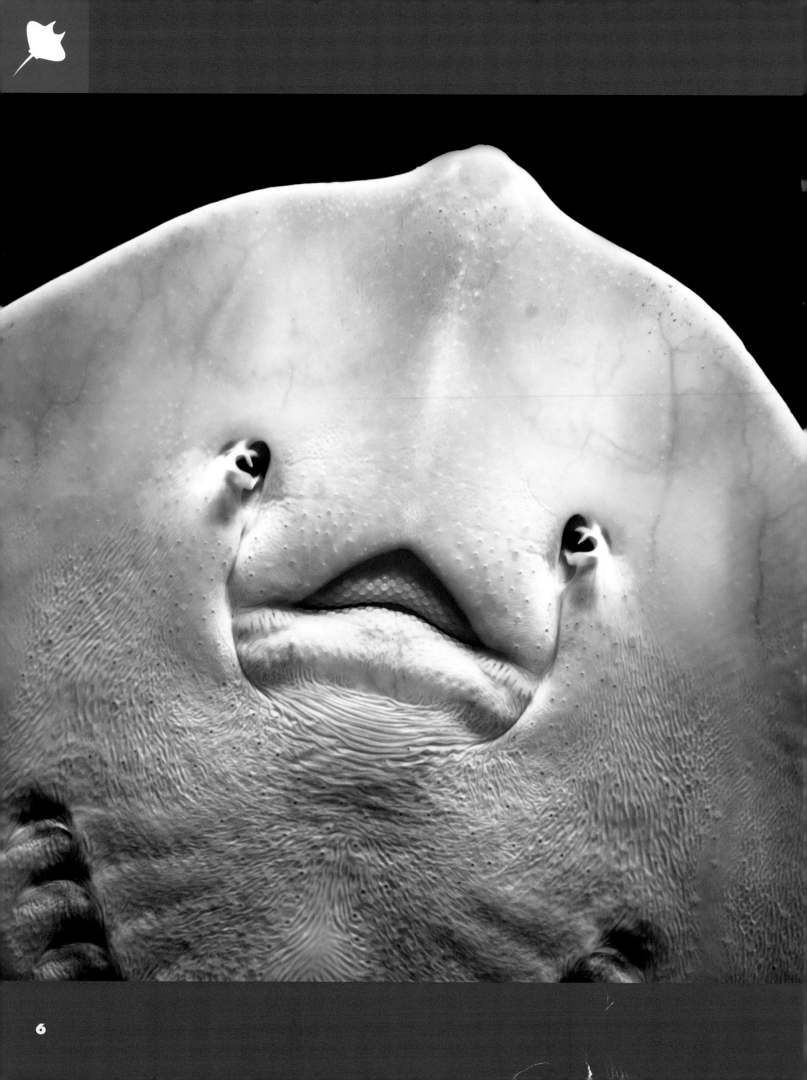

The nostrils are above the mouth, with gill slits below

Rays do not have bones. Instead, their skeleton is made of **cartilage**. A ray's flat body is called a disc. Fins stick out from each side of the disc like wings. A ray's eyes are on top of the body. Its mouth is on the bottom. Most rays are brown, black, or gray.

cartilage a tough, bendy material that is not as hard as bone; human ears are made largely of cartilage

The smallest rays are only four inches (10.2 cm) across. Giant manta rays are the biggest rays. They can be 22 feet (6.7 m) across. They weigh up to 3,000 pounds (1,361 kg). That is as heavy as a small car!

Manta rays typically swim about 15 miles (24.1 km) per hour

Most rays like warm waters. Some rays stay in shallow water. Others swim in deep oceans. A few kinds of rays live in rivers.

Southern stingrays are commonly found in the Caribbean Sea

Adult manta rays eat up to 60 pounds (27.2 kg) of food daily

Some rays eat crabs, clams, worms, and shrimp. Other rays munch on fish, squid, and jellyfish. Some kinds of rays eat tiny **plankton**.

plankton tiny plants and animals that float in the ocean and other bodies of water

*Some kinds of rays
swim in large groups
called schools*

A mother ray gives birth to 1 to 20 **pups** at a time. The pups can swim right away. Most wild rays live 8 to 15 years.

pups baby rays

Some rays move through the water by flapping their fins. Others ripple their fins to swim. If rays stop moving, they sink.

The rippling motion is called undulation, from a word meaning "wave"

*Cleaner fish eat
damaged skin, helping
rays heal faster*

To get clean, rays swim to **reefs** called cleaning stations. Here, small fish eat pests off the rays' skin. Sometimes, the fish even clean the rays' teeth.

reefs ridges of rock, coral, or sand close to the ocean surface

Some people see rays at beaches. Be careful not to step on them! Other people visit rays in zoos. It can be fun to see these strange-looking creatures up-close!

Shuffle your feet through sand to avoid stepping on buried rays

A Ray Story

Why do rays' fins look like wings? People in India told a story about this. They said the myna bird tried to fly across the sea to reach the sun. But the bird got tired. She fell into the water. The **god** of the ocean felt sorry for the bird. So he turned the bird into a sea creature. The bird's legs became a long tail. And its wings became big fins.

god a being that a person or group of people thinks has special powers and controls the world

Read More

Rustad, Martha E. H. *Stingrays*. Minneapolis: Bellwether Media, 2008.

Sexton, Colleen. *Manta Rays*. Minneapolis: Bellwether Media, 2010.

Websites

Enchanted Learning: Manta Ray
http://www.enchantedlearning.com/subjects/sharks/rays/Mantaprintout.shtml
This site has manta ray facts and a picture to color.

National Geographic Kids: Stingray
*http://kids.nationalgeographic.com/animals/stingray/#stingray-swimming
-closeup.jpg*
Learn more about stingrays.

Note: Every effort has been made to ensure that the websites listed above are suitable for children, that they have educational value, and that they contain no inappropriate material. However, because of the nature of the Internet, it is impossible to guarantee that these sites will remain active indefinitely or that their contents will not be altered.

Index

Donated To The Library By

The GFWC Temple Terrace Woman's Club

In Memory Of

Major James E. Cook

©Highsmith® Inc. 1999

Mastering the Art of

HORSEMANSHIP

JOHN LYONS'S Spiritual Journey

Mastering the Art of
HORSEMANSHIP
JOHN LYONS'S Spiritual Journey

by MOIRA C. HARRIS with TAMMY JO LYONS
Photographs by Charles F. Mann

A DIVISION OF BOWTIE, INC.
IRVINE, CALIFORNIA

Nick Clemente, Special Consultant
Karla Austin, Project Manager
Ruth Strother, Editor-at-Large
Michelle Martinez, Assistant Editor
Book design and layout by Michele Lanci-Altomare and Bocu & Bocu

Library of Congress Cataloging-in-Publication Data

Harris, Moira C.
  Mastering the art of horsemanship : John Lyons's spiritual journey /
by Moira C. Harris with Tammy Jo Lyons ; photographs by Charles Mann.
    p. cm.
  ISBN 1-889540-93-5 (hardback : alk. paper)
 1. Lyons, John, 1947- 2. Horse trainers—Colorado—Biography. 3.
Horses—Training—Colorado. 4. Spiritual life—Colorado. I. Lyons,
Tammy Jo. II. Title.

 SF284.52.L97H37 2003
 636.1'0835'092--dc21

2003006967

BowTie Press®
A division of BowTie, Inc.
3 Burroughs
Irvine, California 92618

Printed and Bound in Singapore
10 9 8 7 6 5 4 3 2 1

For Val

TABLE OF CONTENTS

INTRODUCTION

A faint cloud of dust kicks up in the corral, filtering through the late afternoon shafts of sunlight. A young gelding, no more than three years of age, lopes around the outer edge, his neck wet with nervous sweat. There are no corners to this corral—just a continuous circle of fence—so the horse cannot hide from the handler.

The man stands in the middle of the round pen, looking every bit an old-time cowboy from his crooked legs to his ice blue eyes. But he doesn't twirl a lasso or try to capture the animal. Instead, he moves toward the horse, and the horse wildly looks about before dashing in the other direction. But this man, without aggression or emotion, simply and subtly starts to direct the horse with his body language. He begins to ask the horse to move in both directions of the corral just by adjusting his posture and stepping into the horse's space. The horse responds and quickly learns that he can do what the man asks him to do, without fear of reprisal. He begins to relax and slow his frantic pace.

The cowboy steps back and the horse slows to a walk and turns inquisitively toward the man. He begins walking in tentative steps until he stands before the man. The cowboy touches the horse's face gently, rubbing along the cheeks, the jawbone, and the forehead. The man takes a step away. The horse begins to follow the man wherever he walks.

Is this a trick, alchemy, New Age "whispering?" It is none of these. For the man is simply communicating with the horse in a nonverbal language that both can understand. The cowboy understands how the horse learns and how he thinks, so that the man can get the right response from him. He has learned to do this without gimmicks, without expensive training gear, without force, coercion, or pain.

This is nothing new. In the fourth century B.C., the most famous of all Greek horsemen, Xenophon, used animal behavior as his barometer for teaching and riding. His centuries-old principles of horsemanship were based on gentling horses in their training while they were taught new movements and tasks.

Most of the enduring images of our American Wild West include bronc busting and breaking, not gentling horses. Even within the last hundred years in America there have been a scant handful of horsemen from days gone by who have incorporated classical training methods and an understanding of equine behavior to achieve perfect harmony with the horse.

The story you are about to read is of one such cowboy. This horseman has been working with horses for more than thirty years. He's trained horses to accept bridle and saddle, he's broken them to ride, and he's taught them to understand a rider's cues. He's taken difficult horses with behavioral problems and made them willing partners. He's trained the untrainable rogues who would have been sent to the slaughterhouse had he not saved them. He's worked with aged equines as well as newborn foals. Most important, he's taught thousands of people a better way of working with their horses. Today this man, John Lyons, is known throughout the world as "America's Most Trusted Horseman."

Chapter

1

LIFE BEFORE
HORSES

Louisville, Kentucky, is known as horse country—
all you have to do is drive down Interstate 264 to Southern Parkway and
you'll catch a glimpse of the twin spires atop the grandstand roof of
Churchill Downs. For decades, Louisville has had the nation's finest
horseflesh pass over its borders. Its annual spring event, the Kentucky
Derby, turns the city into mecca for racing enthusiasts.

In the Louisville of 1947, there were many momentous occasions.
A Thoroughbred named Jet Pilot won the Kentucky Derby by a mere
head. Perhaps if he had later become a superstar and written his
legacy with a magnificent racing record and a list of talented off-
spring, people would remember that colt. But his win, while
significant, wasn't the event that would influence the future of the
horse industry in years to come. For in Louisville later that year—on
August 31—just a few miles from Churchill Downs, a baby was born
who would eventually change the way people believe horses should be
trained and regarded. He was named John Michael Lyons by his
parents, Ollie and Margaret.

Ollie was a salesman while Margaret was a housewife—nothing
unusual for the times. Margaret stayed home with her young son and raised
him in a Southern Baptist atmosphere. Religion was a big part of the family's

life, and the family faithfully attended church, read the Bible together, and involved John in their Christian values from the time he was just a wee child.

Kentucky's frigid winters and humid summers were tough on Margaret's little toddler. He was diagnosed with debilitating asthma so acute that he needed to receive daily injections to ensure that his bronchial airways wouldn't constrict and leave him fighting for each breath. Margaret took her baby boy to the doctor repeatedly for new treatments, but they had little effect on his condition. She fretted and worried in between visits and tried to keep little John comfortable when the attacks became severe.

John was five years old when the doctor pulled Margaret and Ollie aside. "Your boy is not going to make it unless you get him to a drier environment," he warned. There were anxious discussions over the next several months, and then it was decided that they would uproot their lives and move to a more arid climate. Two years after the caution from the doctor, Ollie and Margaret transplanted the family to Arizona.

The Lyonses moved to Maricopa County and settled in Phoenix. The dry desert air in the Valley of the Sun was just the ticket for John—it helped deepen the little boy's lung capacity, and he was able to breathe freer. He thrived in spite of summer days with 100-plus degree heat, and his need to be constantly medicated gradually tapered off.

Young John discovered a newfound freedom in his improved health and made a vow to himself that he'd never get that sick again. He became fanatical about sports and played just about every American ballgame there was. He took up baseball in elementary and middle school, since Ollie was a devotee of the sport, and John had a natural affinity for it. He continued to play baseball through high school, and as a teenager, he added basketball and football to his repertoire. He was a natural athletic star, garnering awards in all sports, and was selected to the all-state team in baseball during high school. He even lettered in football and basketball.

But John was not exactly a model student. While he genuinely tried hard and did his homework dutifully, academics didn't come easy for him. He was sought after as a ballplayer, though, and when John was finishing his senior year of high school in 1966, he found out he'd received a scholarship to Phoenix Junior College for two full years. Two years—despite his average grades! John was ecstatic. This could be a turning point, he thought. He threw himself into his studies and found ways that helped him become more successful at his schoolwork. His senior year ended on a great note—and he was on to a college career.

John and his father,
Ollie, in 1960

College was a good time for John. It seemed as though he'd really hit his stride. And he was popular, too—he had loads of friends and acquaintances. Easy with words and charm, John was making the most of his new life, yet he still wanted to focus on getting good grades while having an athletic career. He dated frequently, but wasn't about to get serious about anyone. Since he'd just broken up with his high school sweetheart, Katherine Kwic, after a three-and-a-half-year relationship, he needed to have some time to himself and not be tied down.

John's parents had divorced in 1965, and soon after his mother remarried Richard Rhodes, a businessman who spent a lot of time traveling. He and John got along tremendously, and he was a good influence on the young college student. "I really want you to think about expanding your horizons, John," Richard said. "Look beyond college—see what the future might hold for you." Richard told John to believe in himself and that he could accom-

*Looking back–
John as a boy.*

plish almost anything in his life that he set his mind to. As their relationship grew, John figured out how to act responsibly, while Richard's continual encouragement made him confident that he could accomplish his dreams.

And so things moved along nicely for John in his freshman year at Phoenix Junior College. John was a stellar baseball player. That spring he met Jerry, a fellow player on the team. Jerry had a good sense of humor, and he and John spent a lot of afternoons together after practice just hanging out and having fun. One day when John was over at Jerry's house, John noticed a photo that was hanging on the wall of the living room. In the picture was a pretty blond girl—Jerry's seventeen-year-old sister, Susie, who had a vivacious smile and a lively glint in her eye. John studied

MASTERING THE ART OF HORSEMANSHIP

the photo for several minutes before asking his friend, "Hey, who's this?"

The year was 1968. Jerry introduced the two, and John asked Susie if she'd like to go out. She agreed, and on their first date they went to a movie. There were a couple more dates, but Susie had just split from her high school boyfriend Mike so it wasn't exactly love at first sight. They got along fine and conversation came easy, but sparks didn't fly like they did for her and her former flame. When her old boyfriend stepped back into the picture, Susie broke off dating John and went back to Mike.

John took the opportunity to throw himself back into his studies and became focused on raising his GPA. He majored in education and minored in medicine with the intention of becoming a teacher and coach. In the fall of 1968, he transferred to the University of Arizona in Tucson to play college baseball. That January, Susie and John's paths crossed once again, and she'd broken up with Mike—this time for good. The timing seemed much better, and John and Susie began seeing each other a lot. Their casual relationship took on a more serious tone, and conversations between the two occasionally danced around "the future."

John had been going steady with Susie for a couple months when John's step dad, Richard, made a casual comment that he should get married to her. "It'll help settle you down, John." John thought hard about that over the next few days. Did he need to "settle down?" Was he ready for that responsibility? Did he want to share the rest of his life with her?

A few weeks later, he visited his doctor. "John, you have stomach ulcers. What are you worrying about?" the doctor asked.

"Mainly school. Oh, and sports. I want to be the best," John replied.

His doctor laughed. "Maybe you need someone to take care of you. I can help, but you need to quit fretting and enjoy life, too."

John agreed. Everything around him seemed to be telling him the same thing. He knew the time was right.

He drove over to Susie's house and picked her up. She slid into the passenger's seat and they chattered away about the day's events. At a quiet moment, John slowly said, "Look Susie, it's this way. I like you, you like me. Do you want to get married?"

Susie took her eyes briefly off the road to glance over at John sitting next to her. She paused for a moment, cocked her head, smiled, and replied, "Yeah, okay."

It was that simple. They went back to his house that evening and talked about marriage and their future. They talked about what John wanted in a wife, what Susie was looking for in a husband, and came to a basic agreement.

Susie said, "It would be great if I didn't have to work, because what I really want to do is raise a family. You know, having kids, maybe four, would be perfect."

"Well, I was kind of thinking maybe six kids, but hey, I can compromise," he said. They went over the calendar and set a date to get married. All John had to do was finish his senior year in college.

At the time, John was working part-time as a basketball coach for a Catholic grade school. Prior to taking on the job, the team had never had a winning season, but that year he took them to a city championship. That made the administration at Southpoint High School the largest high school in Tucson, Arizona, sit up and take notice. Once John finished his last year at the UA, he'd have his bachelor's degree. A staff member at Southpoint called to say that if he continued his graduate work to get his master's degree, they would give him a head

MASTERING THE ART OF HORSEMANSHIP

basketball—and baseball—coaching job. That clinched the deal for John and Susie. They were set for a promising future.

The wedding date was just on the horizon. A couple of weeks before the big day, John went out and rented a small apartment in town. He spent his free time getting it ready for his new bride, moving in all their things and arranging the furniture as good as any young bachelor/coach could do. Together they slapped on a fresh coat of paint and both became excited to begin life as husband and wife.

It was funny the way that Susie and John started their lives together on August 23, 1969. Theirs was a partnership at first—a friendship. Neither one was madly, passionately in love with the other. Susie was right for John because she had all the qualities that he liked in a person who would be the mother of his kids. It would be a couple of years later that they would actually fall in love with each other and feel that romantic passion that lovers share.

The Lyonses had a beautiful wedding. Resplendent in white, Susie beamed happily throughout the ceremony, and John was delighted with his decision to get married when they did. As a wedding present, Richard and Margaret sent them on a honeymoon to Hawaii for two weeks. They had a glorious time on the islands, playing on the beautiful white sandy beaches, exploring the lush tropics, and luxuriating in the plush hotels. But John had a million things racing through his head right before the wedding. At first he tried to ignore the little voice in the back of his mind, but the voice got louder each day. It kept saying that he didn't want to go through two more years of college to be a teacher and work for $15,000 a year. He didn't think that he'd be satisfied with his life. While on their honeymoon he told Susie what he was thinking. "I don't want to go back to school for two more years. I'd really rather get a job when we got back home. What do you think?"

Susie was fine with this change of heart and plans, and being young and pretty carefree herself, she didn't see what the big deal would be if he didn't return to get his master's degree. They flew back home to Phoenix four days early, as John was anxious to find a job and start working.

Richard, John's stepfather, owned a 3,000-acre cotton farm just outside of Phoenix, and he agreed to put John to work. Each day, John rose well before the sun came up so that he could start his job at 5:00 A.M. His day ended late, and he often didn't get back to the small apartment he shared with Susie until 7:00 or 8:00 at night. He worked every day of the month, getting only one day off per month to spend with his new bride. He never saw Susie during the daylight hours other than during that one day off. His earnings were meager. The newlyweds had basically $400 dollars a month to live on. John set aside $15 a week for groceries, but the rest went to the apartment rent and other bills.

When Susie wasn't with her friends or visiting her mom, she spent a lot of time alone in the apartment waiting for John to get home. On an impulse, Susie went to an animal shelter and adopted a small mixed-breed puppy, with longish light brown fur and big eyes. John was a little annoyed—the dog's adoption fee was $15—and so their week's grocery money was gone. But Susie loved the dog and was terribly lonely in the house by herself, so John let her keep the puppy. "She's such a sweet thing," said Susie. "I'm calling her Buffy."

November rolled around, and John had been working for about three months. Thanksgiving was only days away, and Susie's mom helped the young couple by buying them a turkey. "I'm so excited," she told her mother. "Since it's our first Thanksgiving together, I want to do it all up

right." John was working so hard every day, and she knew how much he was looking forward to a marvelous meal—especially the leftovers: sandwiches with thick slices of carved turkey and mayo. He took a brown-bag lunch to work, so he would have a great lunch every day for a week.

Throughout Thanksgiving Day, the bird slowly roasted in the oven, filling the small apartment with succulent aromas. Finally, it was time to enjoy the perfection of the turkey and all of its trimmings. After finishing their early dinner, Susie and John pushed away from the table and decided to go to the movies, leaving the leftovers on the counter. When they returned to the apartment, they found Buffy lying stiffly on her side, her belly huge and distended, breathing in labored breaths. The dog had eaten the entire turkey carcass. There went their leftovers.

To make matters worse, the dog's life was in grave danger. Susie thought the dog was going to die, and that they'd killed her by leaving

MASTERING THE ART OF HORSEMANSHIP

temptation on the counter. "I didn't even know she could jump that high!" Susie wailed. John dashed to the phone and called the small animal clinic. The vet on duty said, "Well, there's really nothing you can do. She'll either make it or she won't. You'll just have to give her time." John hung up the phone and shook his head.

But Buffy didn't die. In fact, later that night she started passing all the turkey she ate, crapping everywhere in the apartment. There were land mines the size of cow patties, which John and Susie had to clean up. The next day, Buffy was no worse for wear, but because their weekly budget was used for Thanksgiving and vet bills, the family lived on pork and beans for the next week.

Six months after John started working on the cotton farm, he decided that he wasn't cut out to be a farmer, irrigating fields, picking cotton, and fixing farm equipment. He had been working extremely hard, but brought home little money and he never got to see his pretty wife. He'd have to figure out something else.

His next step was to become an insurance salesman. He left the job on the cotton farm, where he had been slaving for twelve hours each day, thirty days a month, to suddenly find himself strolling on one of Phoenix's many lush golf courses, talking and schmoozing with clients. He made small talk with all kinds of people so that he could find out what their insurance needs were. Where he once had no time during the day, now he found himself with plenty—in fact too much. Plus, he detested trying to drum up business, pestering his friends and relatives to buy a policy.

He had been working for about two weeks, trying to sell insurance to his high school friends, when one of the guys he used to play ball with told him how profitable his job was selling furniture at Levitz. Even better, his friend told him that all the top salesmen got manufacturer's reps jobs offered to them. He encouraged John to apply for a job.

John did and was hired. Susie was ecstatic—maybe things were on their way up. And they were—John ended up being one of the top sales-men on the floor in the first year of employment. He went from struggling to make rent and pay bills with $400 a month, to bringing home more than three times that salary. John was able to buy Susie little presents and take her out to dinner every week.

They even had enough money to consider buying a house. New housing tracts were springing up in all the suburbs of Phoenix, so John and Susie would spend weekends driving around Scottsdale, Chandler, and Mesa, looking at sparkling model homes. They bought a little two-

bedroom house, brand-new in the tract, that cost $15,400. It had a nice view of Camelback Mountain. To enjoy the backyard, they put in a screened-in porch.

After they were settled, Susie began yearning for a baby. John told her that they didn't have enough money to have a child yet but said that if she got a job and earned enough money to pay for the doctor and hospital bills, that they would start their family. Susie said she'd get a job, and, like clockwork, became pregnant. The young couple told their moms and dads, who were thrilled to hear that they were going to be grandparents. For eight months, a pregnant Susie worked at a fast-food restaurant. The lean days of the cotton farm were well behind them, and the Lyonses were set up for a comfortable life.

Meanwhile, John was such an amiable salesman for Levitz that he was able to get customers to make additional purchases such as buying

MASTERING THE ART OF HORSEMANSHIP

bedding when they bought a bed. He sold more of EB Malone Bedding products than anyone in the store, and the company knew it. True to his friend's word, manufacturer representative jobs were offered to those who did well, and soon John received a phone call. EB Malone's office asked him to be the company's Dallas, Texas, representative. John really didn't want to move to Dallas since he didn't exactly have the $1,100 to move their belongings, and they'd just settled into the new house. The company agreed to pay John back for his expenses if he stayed in Dallas for six months. He would just have to come up with the cash up front, and in half a year, he'd get reimbursed. So he went to his mom, who had the money in the bank, to see if she would loan the money to Susie and him.

His mom thought quietly, then said, "No, honey, I'm not going to do that."

"But why? You know I would pay you back," said John.

"Because you'll always know that I'm available to help out," she replied, "and you won't develop any independence on your own. What you've got to learn to do is find the money without me, so then you'll always be able to manage on your own."

John was pretty angry. It wasn't like he was being lazy or just asking for a free handout. He wanted to take the Dallas job because the money was going to be good—he'd be able to pay her back quickly. But he bucked up and didn't press her on her decision. Instead he thought about what he could do. He decided to sell some shotguns that he didn't really need and borrowed a little from a friend. He then had enough to accept the job and start making arrangements for the move.

Susie's pregnancy was fairly easy on her. Her baby girl was born on November 14, 1970, and they named her Tammy. Baby Tammy was going to be only two months old when they were scheduled to head to Texas. The moving company picked up their furniture and put it all in the shipping van. Susie and John spent the next few days getting ready for the big journey.

On New Year's Eve that year, John and Susie were alone in their empty house. All of their friends were out celebrating, and the rest of the family all seemed to be doing something else. Staying in with his new baby, John's mind was a million miles away, thinking about Texas, about how he was just twenty-three and his whole life was taking a new and unknown path. Even though John was with his wife and little girl, both he and Susie felt that it was the loneliest night ever.

Dallas, however, turned out to be a good career move. Within a year, John was offered the promotion of plant manager if he moved to Cincinnati.

*The Lyons's home in
Lenexa, Kansas.*

Since both he and Susie had been brought up in the dry, hot climate of
Arizona, they were a little concerned about moving even farther east, away
from their families and all that was familiar. But the promotion was too
good to pass up. It was a tough decision, but John decided that it would be
a positive move overall.

On moving day, they loaded the car and headed up the highway with little
Tammy in her car seat. John drove for hundreds of miles, until they reached
the Tri-State area and eventually, Cincinnati. The sedan rolled under a cold,
gray sky, and the hills and trees made the valley look gloomy. John looked at
the place where they'd make their new lives and swallowed hard. He might
not be used to the cold, wet Ohio winters, but he was willing to give it a try.

Cincinnati, like Dallas, turned out to be a boon as well. Susie became
pregnant again, and within a year, their second-born, Sandy, arrived. Life
was happily continuing on an upward trend.

MASTERING THE ART OF HORSEMANSHIP

John's brother-in-law, Larry Gross, was a medical rep for Richards Company, an orthopedic supplier in St. Louis, Missouri. The family knew that John was quickly moving up in the world, and he had proved to be a savvy businessman and manager. When Larry found out that there was an opening for a sales position in Kansas City, Kansas, he told John to fly in for an interview.

"Why would I do that?" said John. "Look, I'm twenty-three, I run this big plant, and I've got a salesman working for me. There are twenty employees at the plant, and I'm making good dough—more than twenty thousand a year here. Why would I move now, when things are going so great?"

"Because you can make fifty grand a year," Larry said.

"I'll be there next week."

The Richards Company eagerly offered John the position, but the job didn't start for nine months. He moved to St. Louis early and worked with his brother-in-law so that he could learn the trade, the product line, and how to deal with his physician clients.

John was a quick study since he had taken several medical classes at the University of Arizona. His physical education courses, such as human anatomy, physiology, and zoology, were basically premed classes. After his training, John and the family made the relatively short move to Kansas City. He hit the ground running, and found that he could do really well in the industry. At the end of his third year in Kansas City, he was working only three days a week yet bringing home $100,000 a year.

Land was plentiful outside of the suburbs where they had settled, so they bought a nice 5-acre piece of property just outside of Lenexa, Kansas. Hardly a ranch, the acreage was basically some land that had a little bit of pasture encircled by a barbed wire fence. Still, it was land, and it was theirs.

John believed that anyone who had that kind of land ought to have a horse to put on it. He started looking in the classified section of the local newspaper under Horses for Sale. He saw one that sounded like a perfect deal: "Gelding, twelve-years old. With saddle and tack box. Take all for $350."

That weekend, John drove over to take a look at the horse. Ike was a nice quarter horse gelding, well broke and kind-hearted. John rode him and liked the horse, so he told the owner that he'd take him and made arrangements for the horse to be delivered to his property.

John took to horse ownership instantly. He'd ridden horses before but had never really dealt with the day-to-day aspects of living with them.

Since there was no shelter, he built a winter barn for Ike, as well as a space to store his hay and tack. He enjoyed going out in the morning to feed Ike, cleaning out the corrals, and saddling up and going for afternoon rides. Ike was a good-natured guy, and John learned more every day, as many new horse owners do, how to care for his new friend.

Not long after he got his horse, John was driving to work one day and saw a man riding alongside the road. John slowed down to get a good look at the horse and rider. The horse was a tall dark bay. She had a beautiful head and moved swiftly. As the horse and rider traveled down the road, John noticed that the horse was neither cantering nor trotting, but using a good ground-covering gait. They were flying down the road, yet the rider's hat didn't bounce at all—they seemed to be gliding as they went. John slowly pulled over to the side of the road and got the rider's attention.

"Hey, what kind of horse is that? She's really neat," asked John.

"She is a Tennessee walker," the rider replied.

"How much does one of those horses go for?" he asked.

"Well, about $500," said the rider.

"I'll take her," said John.

"Well now," the rider said, "I don't think so. I mean, she is for sale, but first you have to show me if you can ride this kind of horse. My name's Tom. Tom McNeal," he said.

Tom's home was only a couple of blocks away at the top of the hill. He told John to drive up and meet him there, and he would let John ride in his backyard.

When Tom arrived, he dismounted and led the horse into the ring. John got up in the saddle. He picked up the reins and squeezed the horse, who immediately went into her running walk. John found the ride smooth and amazing. He sat the horse well and liked the responsiveness. Tom smiled. "Okay then, John. I'll sell her to you then."

They chatted for a bit while Tom showed him around the rest of the barn to see his other horses. They walked over to a lovely mare the color of jet black with only a splash of white between her eyes. The mare, Misty, was full of fire and spirit, but Tom treated the horse like she could talk—scratching her face and murmuring affections to her. "This lady's my favorite on the property," said Tom.

When John came by later to pick up his new Tennessee walker, Tom told him, "You know, if you ever want to go out riding, you just come on over here. You sit that horse well."

Kicking up dust with Misty.

Tom and John became fast friends. They rode together regularly; they drank together, and talked about horses. Tom imparted his wisdom and experience to John, who soaked it all up. They loved to schedule long rides at the end of the workday and would often ride into the night, trading stories and jokes. John eventually talked Tom into letting him buy Misty two years later. The mare soon became one of John and Susie's favorites as well.

Susie loved their home in Kansas City. It was a gorgeous modern three-level home in a great neighborhood. She was a natural at decorating, and she filled the house with beautiful furnishings. Her husband was successful at his job, they had plenty of friends in their community, and she and her girls had many pleasures in their life. Afternoons for the Lyonses were often filled with neighborhood rides on the horses and softball games at the park. It was the perfect suburban lifestyle.

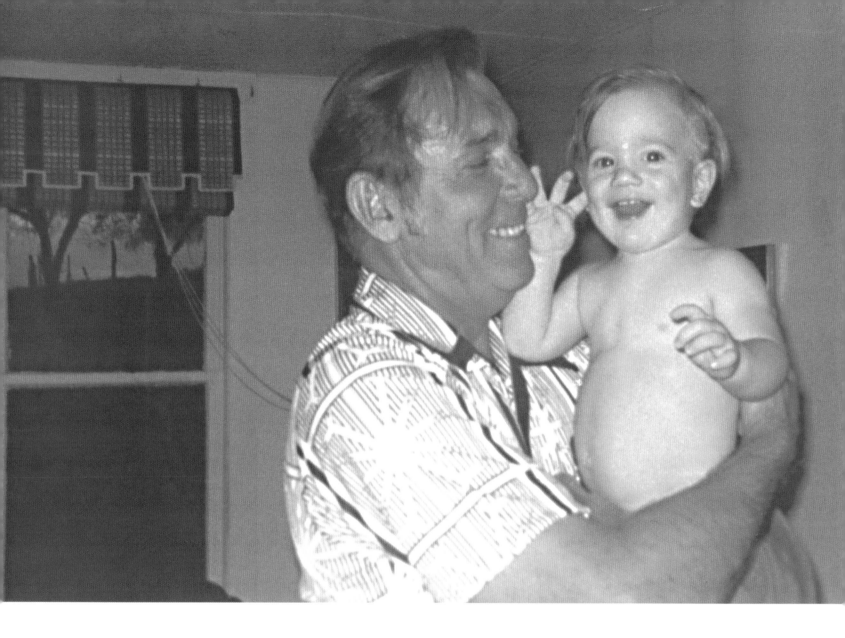

Josh with his Papa Ollie in 1976.

It was 1975 and John had been working at his job for more than three years. He began to feel slightly unsettled, perhaps just a bit claustrophobic. There was increasing pressure on him as a salesperson, and he was a little discontented with himself and his career choice. He didn't want to look back at his life when he was fifty years old and regret settling for a job just because of its ample salary. He needed fulfillment, and he wasn't getting it from the nice house and a safe, secure sales job. He wanted to try something new, but could he attempt to make the change? He knew he didn't want to farm—he had been down that road. But he did truly want to live in the country. He was still young—just twenty-seven, and began to realize he needed something more than money to be content. He didn't fear out-and-out failure, because it was a bigger deal for him to regret not taking a chance, than to take a chance and not succeed.

John thought about the things that gave him pleasure and the lifestyle that he really cherished. After a day's work, he liked to unwind down at the barn with the horses. He found himself spending extra time at his 5-acre property, just mucking out stalls and thinking about what he wanted to do with the next part of his life. He loved the relationship he had with his horses and tried to think of ways that he could make his work as fulfilling as his horse time.

John and Susie decided to build a house by the barn. He talked to an architect in town and together they discussed the details of the floor plan. The new building plans for the house weighed on his mind, especially when he was at the barn or out riding, alone with his thoughts. He became a little fretful about his job, which despite making life comfortable, did little for his soul. His spirit was yearning for something more. At this time Susie was pregnant with their soon-to-be son. Susie seemed to pick up on John's anxiety, and ended up delivering the baby two months early; Josh was in the hospital for the first month of his life. It seemed that life was taking a stressful turn.

John's ten-year high school reunion was coming up, and he was excited to go back home to Phoenix and see old friends and his family. In May 1976, he packed up Susie, the girls, and young Josh, and they made the two-day drive to Arizona. The reunion was a good time for him to catch up with everyone and see what was new with the rest of the family. He spent a long time with his mom, since she was a wealth of information and inspiration. And from his mom he found out that Lenny, John's stepbrother with whom John had worked on the cotton farm, had just bought a ranch in Bond, Colorado.

"Really? You know, I kinda was thinking about moving out of the city, maybe trying something different," John confided.

"Well," she said encouragingly, "Why don't you drive back home to Kansas City by going through Colorado? Lenny would be glad to see you."

So on their return to Kansas City, they drove up north to Lenny's ranch. Liking what he saw in Colorado, John's route meandered here and there. Susie slept in the passenger's seat, while the kids played in the back. John could barely keep his eyes on the road, with the mountains rising up majestically from the canyon. He was in awe of the gorgeous scenery, the colors that danced in the sunlight, and the wildness of the valley.

John nudged Susie awake and said, "I have found home. I'm not leaving Colorado."

2

A NEW LIFE IN COLORADO

No one expected John to come home one day and announce that he wanted to be a cattle rancher and a cowboy, and to live in Colorado. But the visit to Lenny's ranch only solidified his desire to move, and during his short time there, he fell more in love with the state of Colorado. John confided in Lenny, "I really want to move out of the city, Lenny. Do you know of any ranches close by for sale?"

Lenny told him that he'd actually been talking to the family next door to his place, the Horns, and they were thinking about selling their place. John was excited—maybe he and Lenny could have adjoining ranches! Eventually, the Horns decided to stay put, but John was undaunted. It just meant he'd have to search elsewhere. It was as if he had a new lease on life, even upon his return to Kansas City.

He talked to Susie about his new dream of moving, of giving up his sales job to try his hand at a rural life. Susie looked around her beloved suburban house, her eyes welling up with tears. She didn't want to leave all this behind! It was a huge upheaval for the Lyonses, and each argued his and her side. Susie cried for days, not wanting to accept that change was on the horizon.

John tried to tell her, "Things will be okay with a new start, honey—you'll still have the quality of life that you have right now, here in Kansas

City." And Susie didn't want to be completely unreasonable because she did love being John's wife and the mother of his kids. Conveying what a new start would mean to him, John eventually got Susie to acquiesce. She'd just become a born-again Christian, and she felt in her heart that maybe *this* was God's plan for her life with John. Her newfound faith ultimately gave her peace about the move. With John being so intent on changing their lives, Susie could only hope that this truly was the best for their family.

Meanwhile, the rest of the family was up in arms about the situation. John's father, Ollie, screamed at him, "Are you crazy? Look at all you're giving up!" Others, from neighbors to coworkers and clients, echoed this sentiment. He was nuts to give up a six-figure job to go into the middle of nowhere, to live on a ranch and raise cattle—a vocation that he knew absolutely nothing about. "It's the dumbest thing you can do," friends said. "You don't want to get into the business of ranching. How can you walk away from everything you've built here?"

The family tried an intervention of sorts, cloaked under the guise of a family outing. John's brother-in-law Larry and John's sister Anna had a sprawling house on the Lake of the Ozarks, in Missouri, so Susie and John headed up that way for a long weekend. They were under the assumption that it was a real family get-together, since John's dad was also going to be there. John didn't know it was the family's last-ditch effort to talk some sense into him.

Everyone ganged up on him, sitting him down in the living room and imploring him to listen to reason. After all, who leaves a job that is so secure for a life that is far from stable and wonderful? But John was completely determined. And surprisingly, Susie was by his side, supporting him. With Christ now in her life, she was more accepting of John's dream. The other members of the family collectively shrugged their shoulders and finally gave up.

Since the Horns weren't selling their place, John began looking for other ranch property on Colorado's Western Slope near Grand Junction. In August 1976, John found a 500-acre cattle ranch with a seventy-five-year-old farmhouse to purchase outside the small town of Silt, up from the Divide Creek area. The Lyonses sold the house in Kansas City, and Susie and John once again made arrangements for movers. John made a couple trips to Lenny's ranch, in Colorado, moving all of the barn equipment, horses, and trucks and trailers. Around November or so, the family began to pack up the furniture and furnishings, clothes, and the

John and Susie's ranch in Silt, Colorado, during the winter.

kid's' toys. The moving truck came to take all their things. With Tammy Jo, Sandy, and new baby Josh in tow, the Lyonses left for the long move to Colorado. Susie was concerned about the trip since fragile little Josh was only nine months old and had spent his first month in the hospital's preemie ward.

The drive was interesting, since winter was well on its way. Susie observed the changing landscape, from the flat Midwestern plains of Kansas, to the rolling untamed mountains, where snowy peaks jutted out from their rocky basin. Each mile that they traveled took them through more and more remote towns until they reached Silt, population nine hundred.

The furniture movers hadn't arrived yet when the Lyonses pulled up the dirt drive to the ranch house. To make matters worse, escrow hadn't closed yet, so John had to drop off Susie and the kids and immediately

MASTERING THE ART OF HORSEMANSHIP

drive to Denver some 180 miles away to take care of the paperwork. The Denver trip would take about five hours one way, so John was hoping to be able to do the trip in one day. Susie waved good-bye from the porch, clutching little Josh in her arms. She then turned and walked into the house. Her shoes echoed on the creaky floors, amplifying the hollow emptiness of the house. It was getting cold, too. Susie hoped that John would be able to tie up all the loose ends quickly and come back home early.

But John didn't return that night—there were still a few roadblocks before escrow could close. Susie was all alone in the big, empty farmhouse. She was without a vehicle, and even if she had had one, the nearest store and gas station was 15 miles away. The house had a coal furnace that required stoking and she tried vainly to remember how to work it from the crash course she'd received from the real estate agent. But she was at a loss. It was nightfall, and she was cold and terribly worried about the baby whom she kept warm in her arms. Luckily, a neighbor, noticing signs of life around the house, came over and helped her turn on the heat. Susie was grateful for his help. But still, she did not have her furniture; no bed, no refrigerator. It was cold enough so that she could keep the milk and formula on the porch outside. She slept fitfully that night. This was not the start of the new life that she had hoped for. John returned after three days. He pulled into the driveway just as the movers were unloading the sofa.

That was how life began on the cattle ranch for the Lyonses. And instead of it getting easier after those first days, new and different challenges were thrown their way—something neither one bargained for. John bought 104 head of cattle to start with, but he had few clues about successful ranching. He picked up his cattle knowledge day by day. He had no idea what a heifer is, or what the term "*first calf heifer*" means, or even what the difference between a cow and a heifer or a steer and a bull is. But he started to find out, and he learned quickly—he had to.

He had more than 400 acres that needed irrigation, but first he needed to remove all the cow manure in the pastures left from the previous ranching operation. He was able to put his cattle on Bureau of Land Management (BLM) forestland while he prepared his fields. But John didn't have a clue on how to harrow. He didn't even own a proper tractor yet. He looked at his options and came up with the idea of attaching an old metal box spring to a rope and dragging it behind his Chevy Blazer. He started up the Blazer, box spring groaning and protesting loudly, and put the truck in drive.

A nearby neighbor, John Bolton, noticed the large clouds of dust that were being kicked up by John's contraption. He drove over to watch and leaned against the fence, laughing at John's attempt to work his land. Bolton then went back to his ranch, got in the driver's seat of his John Deere, and drove his tractor and harrow over. The harrow was just a single-disk type, but it was a lot better than John's Blazer-and-box-spring setup. Several days later, John's pastures were harrowed.

In December 1977, John hadn't even been ranching a year, and the climate of the cattle industry was changing rapidly. It had not been a good year for real estate or for the cattle market. Interest rates soared to 19 percent, while the cattle market nearly collapsed with prices dropping to only 120 dollars for a 400-pound calf. That year, John and Susie were witnesses to the hundred-year drought that had been plaguing western Colorado. There was no water, which meant little hay production. Hay prices skyrocketed to $100 a ton, and since it took 2 tons to get one cow through the winter, John was already $80 per cow in the hole—and he hadn't even had one calf on the ground.

However, Nebraska had gotten all the rain that Colorado was supposed to get, so hay was plentiful—belly deep to horses. A cattleman came driving through the Colorado valley to try to get ranchers to bring their cattle to his place in Nebraska. He stopped off at each ranch and gave the cattlemen his pitch: "I can feed and care for them. It would be a lot cheaper for you to bring them to my place." John did some quick math in his head and despite not being a savvy cattleman, he figured it made good economic sense to truck his cattle over to Nebraska and buy hay there at $20 a ton. The rancher agreed to calve John's cattle out, feed, and care for them for a reasonable price. John and Lenny talked this over and decided they would both send their cattle to Nebraska for the winter. The cattle were loaded on a truck and trundled down the road to the neighboring state.

John and Lenny were relieved to have found such a good situation for their cows. Right after the New Year, they drove together to Nebraska to check on the herd. It was supposed to be a quick trip—they were just planning to stop in for a day or two, check in on the cows, then come right back.

They arrived at the farm during a violent ground blizzard. The snowfall was so heavy that John could only faintly make out the house at the end of the driveway. John and Lenny donned their heavy jackets and put up their hoods. Still, the wind fiercely whipped through them, so they

*John working a horse
in the snowy pasture.*

put socks over their ears to keep them warm, and began their fight
against the storm and staggered toward the house.

As they lurched through the snow, John could make out a small
mound on the ground. He looked closer. It was a calf, lifeless and frozen.
There were dead calves everywhere. It looked like a dreadful massacre. It
turned out that the rancher had purchased some yearlings from
Louisiana, and because they had gone from a warm climate to a frigid
one, they had fallen victim to the storm. With each step that John and
Lenny fought to take, they came across another dead calf. John's stomach
turned and he thought he was going to be sick. It seemed like hours
before they reached the porch of the ranch house. John knocked on the
door and the rancher opened the door.

"What are you guys doing here? How on earth did you make it
up here?"

John explained that the truck was up the road, and they had just walked.

He was amazed. "People die out there in this type of blizzard. You are damn lucky you made it up here."

Because it was January, the cows were just starting to calve. But few babies were surviving. John and Lenny were overwhelmed. They were supposed to be making just a quick trip to see how fat and happy their cattle were, only to discover the herd was in the most grim of winter conditions, just struggling to stay alive. They decided to remain with the calves and cows to make sure that whatever calves they did have made it through the winter.

The first order of business was to save the calves who were already on the ground. John went out to the pasture and picked up a frail, nearly frozen calf and gently carried it up to the house. He laid it down on the kitchen floor so that it could keep warm near the stove. Then he headed back outside into the storm, and found another calf in peril, picked him up, and brought him to the kitchen. Several hours later, the kitchen was full of calves trying to stay alive.

The rancher said that it was the worst winter in seventy years. Either John or Lenny was in the field with the cows, twenty-four hours a day, for a period of thirty days. Working in shifts, they spent thirty-six hours on duty and then took twelve hours off to sleep. The ranch was not set up to feed this many cows in such horrible weather. They had thirty minutes to eat silage, then the next group of cows would be herded in to eat their share. The cattle were constantly searching for a dry piece of ground to stand on, but the entire pasture was nothing but mud.

Because of the harsh winter, they lost ninety calves out of the first hundred cows. The cows were so cold that they could barely maintain their own health, let alone their calves'. So they would end up dropping their calves and walking away from them—not even bothering to lick them off. John and Lenny tried everything that first month. They had to figure out something to save the calves since the storms were rolling in, one after another, and were showing no signs of weakening.

There was a small, dilapidated barn on the premises, and John evaluated its potential to be a cattle barn. On Super Bowl Sunday, John armed himself to clean the barn so they could bring the cows inside to have their calves. John's idea was to keep them out of the wind and snow so that they could bond with their newborns. Once the cows and their calves got stronger, they would be able to go back out into the pasture.

John looked at the floor of the barn. It was covered in manure, so he got his shovel and began to clear it out. He dug and dug; 2 feet down he

John as a young
horseman.

finally hit the bottom. This can't be, he thought. But it was. Even though
it was a small barn, in spots the manure was halfway up to his knees. He
looked up and surveyed the cavernous, hollow building, and realized the
futility of his small effort. Stopping to mop the sweat from his brow, John
thought of the $100,000-a-year job that he had given up, and the nice
warm home filled with family, friends, and laughter. Now he was in the
dead of winter, knee-deep in manure, shoveling out someone else's barn
to save the cows he had spent his last cent on. For several minutes, while
catching his breath, he pondered whether it was worth it.

That was the only time John asked himself that question. It was
worth it, he reminded himself, and he went back to work cleaning out the
barn, methodically removing all the manure from the concrete floor. It
took some time, but he called upon his last bit of strength, and eventually
finished late that night.

While he was shoveling, he knew he had come up with only a short-term solution to his problem. He had realized for some time that the rancher was not managing his cattle well, and John was trying to think of a better way. Ironically, it was the rancher's sister who provided the answer to their troubles. She had riverfront property adjacent to her brother's ranch and had cut 250 tons of hay. But for some reason, it was never picked up to be sold. It just sat out in her field. John came up with the idea to rent the grassy field and put his cows and calves out on it. The cows, John and Lenny reckoned, could fill up on the hay and also lie down in it, so they wouldn't have to fight the cold constantly. With this internal and external insulation, they just might make it through that miserable winter.

Nearby ranchers thought John and Lenny were out of their minds. They said if a storm blew through, which was likely, it would push the cows right into the icy river, and they'd die. John and Lenny did it anyway. No storm hit. A week later the cows who hadn't calved started calving, and lo and behold they began taking care of their calves. And the cold and the wind subsided in the next month. The weather turned slightly better, so in March, three months from the day that they had arrived, they loaded their truck and went home. The cattle were shipped back, and they finished calving out the rest of the herd.

But things were far from completely rosy. Financially, John was a wreck. He and Susie didn't have enough money to even get started—he barely had had enough money to buy the ranch with just enough left over for operating expenses. There was no cash to buy equipment. Now they were into the ranch for a little over a year, yet they were completely broke. Colorado National Bank, the lender for the ranch, hadn't been paid on time. The bank was panicking and it wanted its money. In addition to that, Susie was again pregnant, this time with their fourth child.

Plain and simple, because John had been wiped out by the winter catastrophe, the Lyonses owed the bank more than they could afford to pay. John went in to talk to his lender, explaining the situation. The bank agreed to work with him, and John and Susie started by applying for disaster loans through the FHA. It took John hours each day to fill out paperwork, make telephone calls, and send in applications for loans. He and Susie waited impatiently to see if their loan would get approved. The FHA loan went through, and Colorado National Bank was finally paid off. They also got their operational loan, so that they could get a fresh start.

So John and Susie tried rebuilding their lives. Baby Brandi was born in November of 1978, on Thanksgiving Day. They slowly started to see a profit from the ranch and were able to purchase more equipment to get ready for spring. Then the following winter was a bad one, and this time the poor weather hit Colorado, not Nebraska. Ranchers were losing cattle left and right, just like the year before. Every ranch had the same horror story—cows giving birth to their calves and simply walking away from the weak little newborns.

John, however, had learned a great deal from that horrible Nebraska winter—especially how to keep cows from rejecting their calves in the bitter cold. He'd learned how to graph calves onto cattle, and how to keep them warm. And he was rewarded with his efforts—he had a 99 percent calf crop. His calves were flourishing despite the terrible weather, while other ranchers were having extremely high death losses in their calf crop.

For the next several years, prices for calves were still way down, and interest rates climbed rapidly. The FHA began foreclosing on many different ranches throughout the valley, and that included the Lyons ranch, despite John's grand efforts to keep the ranch afloat. The FHA suggested that John and Susie put the ranch on the market—sell it straight out. John figured that there was a way he could still keep a portion of the land for himself, so he agreed and listed the ranch with an estate agent. Four months later, he had a buyer who actually was going to put down 50 percent toward the mortgage—far more money than John ever had. John would wind up with 40 acres free and clear, as well as one hundred cows and equipment—and $100,000 on top of that. It seemed that everyone would come out ahead: John, the FHA, and the buyer. John once again filled out the reams of paperwork and waited for the transfer. However, it took a year of back and forth with the FHA who was making the buyer go through quite a bit to qualify. Finally, the FHA made the determination that the buyer had too much money and John had emergency loans that could not be assumed by a new buyer. The deal was dead in the water.

If the FHA had determined that in the beginning, John might have been in a better position. But by being strung along for a year, John had eaten up the operating loan and he and Susie were right back to square one. They reapplied for a new loan, but this time the FHA refused and instead talked about foreclosing on the farm within six months. John was forced to sell off his cattle and his farm equipment.

In a bizarre twist, the U.S. government put a moratorium on the FHA, stating that the agency could not foreclose on any more farms and ranches. This put John and Susie in quite a bind. Here he was with his ranch, but no cattle or equipment. He had no way to earn a living. Yet the FHA could not take the ranch back, and John couldn't give the ranch back to the FHA since he owed too much money. He tried to do as much creative financing as possible. He indeed still had his ranch, but he had no income. He didn't want to move into town, but he had to make a living somehow.

Chapter

3

A HORSE ZIPS INTO JOHN'S LIFE

John still had his four horses from Kansas City

while giving cattle ranching a go. In fact, right after John and Susie took up living in Divide Creek in northwestern Colorado, and long before the financial trouble with the ranch, Susie was yearning to do something with horses that was different, a little more special. Lenny had several nice registered Appaloosas that he showed on the Appaloosa Horse Club (ApHC) circuit and had just bought a gorgeous, loud-colored Appy from a ranch in nearby Rifle. Susie decided that she, too, would like a nice horse to show, since she had shown dogs when she was a young girl and loved the atmosphere and competitive nature of the circuit. John talked with his stepbrother and then told Susie, "You know, if you really want to get out there and show horses, we should do it as a family." Since Lenny was such a fan of the Appaloosa breed, John believed it would suit them as well.

On the outskirts of Rifle was the well-known Appaloosa ranch that was owned by C.J. Jackson—the same ranch from which Lenny had bought his fancy Appy. John called Jackson, then he and Susie drove out for a visit. They walked around the ranch, looking at the studs and brood-mares in their pens and watching the foals playing. John turned to Susie and said, "Well, if we're going to buy a nice horse, we might as well make

a little money off him, so why don't we buy a stud?" Of course, later he would realize this was one of the most foolish reasons for buying a stallion, but at the time, it seemed like a brilliant idea laced with practicality.

They looked over the youngsters on the ranch and came across a flashy dark chestnut Appaloosa stud colt with a blanket of white splashed across his rump and a curious look on his freckled face. He was a yearling, born in 1975, and was the half brother to the horse that Lenny had, Zip's Wimpy. As John and Susie examined him, they both fell in love with him immediately. So John paid for the colt and took him back to the ranch.

The colt was named Bright Zip, by Wild Zip out of Mighty Lu. He had fairly nice conformation as a youngster and was registered with the Appaloosa Horse Club, so John and Susie tried showing him at halter in his yearling year. But despite the price tag he came with and his nice disposition, the highest he placed was next to last—and that was only one time. Even some of the other Appaloosas who John had purchased after Zip were doing better at the shows than the stud colt. Yet Susie and John persevered.

For the next year and a half John worked with the horse on the ground. The kids played with Zip, and he was so good-natured that they all took turns climbing on and off his broad back. John even taught him tricks, mainly because Zip was eager to learn and John had to do something while the horse was maturing, since he wasn't stocky enough as a stud to win in the halter ring. He broke him to ride when he was thirty months old, and shortly after that, Susie and John both began training on him.

Zip's even temper made training go pretty smoothly, so the Lyonses thought it would be time to begin showing Zip in events such as western pleasure and trail at local ApHC competitions. A show was coming up in western Colorado, so they figured this would be his under saddle debut.

When they arrived at the grounds, John searched for the show arena. The tiny show ring was housed in a freezing small tin building. People stood cramped in the cold along the arena fence to watch the proceedings. Susie got her entry number and class list while John saddled Zip for his first class: western pleasure. When her event was called, Susie swung into the saddle and rode through the ingate.

Zip looked around the show pen but wasn't alarmed or intimidated. The announcer called for the various gaits—walk, jog, and lope—and Zip did a good job, getting all his leads, carrying himself in a nice frame, and going along at a good rate. He acted like a veteran of the show ring, except for one thing—as Zip loped or jogged along, he whinnied at the top of his lungs. He neighed repeatedly, and his bugling echoed through the tin building. The announcer was hopelessly drowned out, so he simply ceased broadcasting over the PA system. Susie looked at John from the rail, her face crimson, half from embarrassment, half from anger. She wanted to kill John, since he had thought the horse "show ready" when he still had a long way to go.

After that, it was back to the ranch and the drawing board.

More time and effort was needed to settle the young Appy stud, so John diligently worked with him. In addition, John was breaking some ranch horses for Harold and Kay Baumgartner, a local couple from a nearby ranch. John liked using a routine in which he worked the horses first, then took them for a ride down the quiet local country roads.

John had just finished one of the tougher horses, and as a reward, rode him on trails by one of his neighbor's ranches. The farmer was out fixing a fence, so he and John engaged in a quiet conversation. Suddenly, the quiet air was broken by a wild screech. Susie was just cresting the hill on horseback and coming toward them—not in a panic, but at a leisurely walk. Her horse was the one doing the terrible screaming, and it was Bright Zip. Zip continued to whinny and squeal, and as Susie rode by she glared at John, her face dark with mortification. She was still humiliated by the stud's silly behavior at the show, and this screaming, during a quiet trail ride even, was too much. She told John, "I can't stand it any longer. I want to get rid of this horse." John took her aside and soothed her by saying that he would trade her horse for the horse that he was sitting on. And from that day on, Zip became John's horse.

John did get him to stop the histrionics. He used the horse on the ranch to get regular work done, and this made Zip a much more confident, amiable partner. So Zip went back into the show ring. John showed in a variety of classes, such as western pleasure and trail classes, while Susie continued to show him in open jumping and English pleasure. When Zip turned five, John felt that Zip's body had fully matured, that his legs were strong and the bones were completely developed, so he was entered into games classes—speed events where he could show agility and athleticism. John was aiming for the year-end award of high point performance horse, which involved taking him to a series of ten shows. Zip became the high point champion in nine out of ten of those shows.

A turning point came in 1981 when Zip was the High Point Performance Horse of the Year. John and Zip competed at the last show of the

circuit in Vernal, Utah—a really important competition. John was especially looking forward to taking the prize home for high point because a brand-new saddle would be awarded to the winner.

However, Bright Zip and John didn't take home the big prize. Zip lost at the show, and John felt that it was due to foul play and favoritism within the show circuit. He was absolutely fuming—mad at the system, at the politics, and at the lack of objectivity. He tried to quell his anger but couldn't. That night after the show, at 2 A.M., John still couldn't sleep. He got up to take a walk—maybe just shake off the bad mood—and started ambling down the block, not far from the show arena. He began to pray to get control of his anger. As he rounded the corner, he found himself standing in front of a Circle K convenience store that was brightly lit— open twenty-four hours. He looked up at the marquee where specials were usually posted in large black letters. This time, it didn't give the price of a pack of Marlboros or a quart of milk—it said, The Answer Is in Your Change. It was as if God Himself had posted that message for him, and when John stared at the sign, he immediately related this to his situation. Okay, so I'm not going to be able to change the system or show politics, he thought to himself. I just need to make a decision and deal with it. John realized he had to cease being involved in something that he disliked and couldn't change. That day was the last time John rode into the show ring.

But Zip's career was only beginning. When he loped out of the show's limelight, he strode into a different spotlight. Previously, he had led a pretty rigorous schedule, first working on the ranch and then showing full time, not in just one event, but in all, which was sometimes nine to ten classes a day! Besides showing his versatility on the circuit, he had been successful in the breeding shed and was a perfect gentleman around any mare. This résumé—working long hours doing myriad tasks with all kinds of horseflesh— prepared him for a solid future on the road.

John began using Zip to show the public that his training techniques worked and later used him as a demonstration horse at his clinics. But even though John had taught him the ins and outs of demonstrating to the public, Zip didn't exactly take to life as a clinic horse first shot out of the box.

This time it was Zip's turn to teach John—and the lesson was that doing repeated demonstrations of a special leading technique and other maneuvers for an audience could make Zip really sour and cranky. The

more John made Zip go through routines such as the repetitious leading method, the worse Zip acted out. John then realized that the horse-leading technique was to be used sparingly, only when he needed to get extra control. Everyday use became detrimental to his horse's well-being.

Over the next twenty years, Zip taught John many different lessons just by being John's main partner. John trained Zip to trot and canter right up to him when he called; and eventually Zip also learned to free-jump over logs or fences to get to John.

Once he joined John on the clinic and symposium circuit, Zip spent as much time on the road as his owner. His stall would change every few nights for eleven months out of the year. John saw more of Zip than he did of his wife and kids. Sharing the road and a relationship, Zip and John forged a bond deeper than most people have with their families—it was a simple fact that they would always be there for each other.

4

A TURN AT TRAINING

When exactly did John realize that he had a gift

with horses? When did he discover that he wasn't just a good rider, but a trainer with something pretty special to offer?

It was during the late seventies at the Divide Creek Ranch, when one spring day John was out in the lower pasture working Zip before a big show. He'd been riding the horse for the better part of an hour, all the while thinking back to the advice various trainers in the area had offered him on how to make Zip a nicer show horse.

"You should use a tie-down—get that head lower."

"Longe him for about half an hour, so he's not so full of himself."

"Spin that horse in circles, and use a training fork and a wire snaffle on him."

As John assertively schooled Zip, he suddenly believed that he was being heavy-handed with the horse, almost as a result of all the advice he'd received. Some trainers might have thought John wasn't being strong and aggressive enough with the horse, while others might have thought he was out and out too harsh. Regardless, John suddenly realized that enough was enough.

He thought, here I am, frustrated at the way Zip is acting, and what do I do? I'm taking it out on him. I'm going to have to stand in front of God and tell Him why I've dealt with this horse—this good horse—in this way.

Immediately his perspective changed on what he should and shouldn't do when training. He rode Zip out of the pasture and back to the barn, climbed off and unsaddled him. Then he headed into his tack room, got down all the quick stops, running martingales, tie-downs, and fancy bits, and took them to a burn barrel. Pouring diesel fuel on top of the various straps and metal, John lit a match and watched them burn. He reserved one snaffle bit, thinking that if he couldn't learn to train a horse with that mild snaffle, then he should just quit dealing with horses altogether—no training or even riding.

That day led to the biggest change in John's life as far as horses went. He had dozens of horsemen, riders, and trainers all say that he wouldn't get the performance, or be able to teach a horse to do things such as sliding stops, without severe bits or harsh training equipment, but John believed otherwise. It became his quest, and his mantra, to train in a more natural, practical way.

MASTERING THE ART OF HORSEMANSHIP

Horse training helped take John's mind off his financial dilemma: what to do with the ranch now that he had absolutely no cattle, no farming equipment, and no money to get started again. And with each horse he trained, John realized that he relished that partnership.

He was gaining a reputation locally for riding well-trained horses. The family's horses had started out as average mounts with good breeding, but as a result of John's training, they became superlative ranch and show horses. Not only that, his methods proved to be transferable, starting with his immediate family. His girls, Tammy Jo and Sandy, showed in the youth division, and John taught them how to train their own horses before they were ten years old. Word got around in the industry, and folks were quite impressed to see the whole family in the show pen, winning all kinds of awards such as High Point Champion and All-Around Performance Horse. Of course, Zip was the cream of the crop, and people looked at the relationship between John and Zip and desired that with their own horses.

For the time being, John reckoned he'd take in some horses to train. He began this new venture by offering his services to local horsemen and women. When he realized that he could make more money by branching out, he decided to formalize his training as a business.

"I'm going to have to make a price list," he told Susie.

"How about offering to train show horses? Show people will pay more to have their horses ready to go in the arena," Susie said. Together they sat in the kitchen, both with legal pads, and started putting together a flyer, complete with rates that people could pay for his services.

His starting price was $150, for which John would start the horse under saddle, as well as guarantee that the horse would be able to walk, trot, lope, back up, and go through a variety of trail obstacles. If a customer paid him $300, John would add lead changes and western pleasure training to the mix. An owner who wanted a more versatile show horse would pay $600 and receive a horse who would be ready for western pleasure, trail classes, and western riding. John even had a deal for anyone who really thought he or she had a top prospect—he'd train him to be high point performance horse–caliber for $1,200. John didn't have any interest in showing all those horses, but he was certainly eager to train them.

Business started rolling in slowly but steadily. Word spread that there was a trainer who was breaking horses quickly and effectively but without violence or pain.

His training didn't get noticed only locally. Back in his hometown of Phoenix, the horse community there also caught wind that John was

In John's Words

I'd gone to a training clinic and really wanted to learn, so that gave me an idea for my own clinics. We gave the first one right in Silt at a friend's place. Jesus once said a prophet is never recognized in his or her own land. That's why if a prophet goes to another country, all of a sudden he's more important. So I figured just the opposite. If I could put on a successful clinic—admission free— where everyone knew me and showed horses with me, then I could be successful anywhere. One fellow whose horse I worked with was so excited at the end of the day with what we'd accomplished that he wrote me a $50 check. That check was like $100,000 to me. It was so much money to our family at that time. The funny thing was that he was SO excited, he even forgot to sign the check. Nevertheless, we figured at that point that we could be successful in the horse training business.

offering training services for starting show horses. Dr. James Reinhart, a general practitioner, owned an Arabian ranch just outside of Phoenix. He was one of the first to call.

"I was wondering if you'd come out to my place, and I'll get some customers for you. You can work on multiple horses and teach us what you're doing so that we know how to work with our own horses." John asked Susie if she wouldn't mind if the whole family traveled to Phoenix. "We can see all our friends and relatives while we're there," he told her. "The kids can spend time with our parents." The whole clan headed south to Arizona, and over to Dr. Reinhart's place.

When John arrived at Dr. Reinhart's, he found that it wasn't exactly a hub of activity like he thought it would be. Instead of having dozens of horses ready for training, and about the same number of spectators, there was only a pair of Reinhart's Arabians waiting. He walked to the round

MASTERING THE ART OF HORSEMANSHIP

pen, hoping to see an anxious crowd gathering. Instead, his only observer leaning on the rail was an old drunk.

But John had a job to do, so he went to see the horses, both quite different in personality. One was a young gelding, smart and willing. He was a piece of cake to work with. The other was an Arabian stallion. He was extremely beautiful but had a strange, unmanageable streak to him.

John got the stud out and began to saddle him up. He placed the saddle on the horse's back and reached underneath to cinch him up. As John tightened the cinch, the horse craned his neck around and latched onto the saddle, trying to pull the saddle over his head. When that failed, he reared back and broke away, then dashed around the pen at a gallop. He finally sank to his knees and tried to get out of the pen by crawling under the fence.

Most trainers would have seen that horse as berserk or maybe horribly stubborn. John didn't know exactly what to think at the time—but the first

John with Dr. Reinhart's horse.

step was to try to figure out why the horse was behaving so strangely. John began his usual method of running the horse around the round pen to control three things: speed, direction, and change of direction. He did this not only to give the horse something to focus on rather than trying to escape but also to slowly let the horse know that even if his mind didn't want to do what John wanted, eventually his heaving lungs would convince him otherwise. It was a way to establish pecking order without horse or trainer getting hurt.

John thought that maybe patience or shorter training sessions might make the horse respond better to him. And both did. Within a few hours of methodical short sessions with breaks in the middle, he swung into the saddle and rode the stallion around the pen. The Arabian was highly responsive, and John could tell that he was intelligent and quick to learn—although he was far from being a safe horse. John rode him the following day and saw that Reinhart had his hands full. The horse

MASTERING THE ART OF HORSEMANSHIP

remembered what he had been taught but was still exhibiting some odd and dangerous behavior. Still, Reinhart was impressed. "John, I haven't been able to do anything with that crazy stud. What would you charge me to ride this horse for the next two weeks?"

John thought he might as well ask for the moon, since he didn't really think Reinhart would take him up on it. "I'd charge $100 a day."

"You got yourself a deal," said Reinhart.

So every day, John came back to ride, and every day the scenario was the same. He would saddle the stallion and each time he put his foot in the stirrup to mount, the horse would reach back and try to bite John. He practically tried to eat him right off the saddle. However, once John was in the saddle for a while, he couldn't teach the horse quickly enough. The stallion caught on immediately to subtle cues and weight shifts. He executed lateral movements and understood lead changes. But no matter which way John handled the horse before getting on, at a certain point in the training session, almost to the minute, the stud would seemingly go insane and attempt to attack his rider.

John asked Reinhart to stick around and watch one day. "All I'm going to do is get on him and then take him out of the ring and into the field. Keep an eye on your watch, Dr. Reinhart. In an hour, watch what happens with this horse." John rode the horse into the field and began to just walk him, because he had wondered if maybe he might've worked him too hard during all the prior practice sessions.

Reinhart looked at his watch from time to time. The horse looked wonderful—obedient, yet full of vigor. Then sixty minutes passed. Suddenly, the stud reached around and tried to bite John so swiftly and hard that he clamped his mouth down on the stirrup. The horse, not realizing that he was caught on the stirrup, panicked, spun, twisted, and flipped over. Luckily, John flung himself off before the horse hit the ground. Both got up and John reached the horse, grabbed the reins, and led him up to Dr. Reinhart.

"I have no idea what I'm doing wrong, but I know for sure that I'm not helping your horse."

"Why do you say that?"

"Because I don't know how to fix this. There's obviously something I'm doing wrong."

"It's okay, John," said Dr. Reinhart, smiling and absently patting the stud. "We haven't been able to figure it out for the entire time we've had this horse. Sometimes these Arabians are like this. I'll just wait until you come back here next year."

As John looked at the Arabian stud standing by him calmly, with no hint of the extreme temper tantrum that he'd just thrown, he thought, Oh no...I don't want to see this crazy horse ever again!

But John didn't want to quit on Reinhart, or the Arabian. He was sure that he could find the one key that would unlock the mystery to the horse's behavior. After he put away the horse for the day, he continued to observe him while he was alone. The horse stood quietly for several moments in his run-in shed. Then John watched as the stallion leaned against one of the shed's support posts, squealed, and reached back and bit himself, as if he were latching on to another horse he was fighting. He repeatedly raked his flesh with his own teeth. John watched in morbid fascination. He could sort of understand if a horse attacked humans, but one who bit himself?

John had heard about this self-mutilation behavior. It was known as a stereotypy, commonly called a vice. It is classified the same way as stall weaving, cribbing, and wind sucking—but this was the most extreme of all stereotypical behaviors. His heart went out to the poor horse who would forever be troubled by his own brain chemistry, his own genetics.

Dr. Reinhart's ranch was situated right next to another Arabian breeder. John went over to see the trainer since he had a full brother to the stud. The trainer was candid with John. "Yeah, we had the full brother. We worked for six months in order to get that colt broken to ride. We even thought that gelding him would change things, but it didn't. We had to sell him as an unbroken horse. It hadn't mattered that we had ever climbed up on him—he was as unbroke as the first day we ever worked him. Of all the horses I've ever had, that was the one that I couldn't ever do anything with."

John was perplexed. "Why do you think he was that untrainable?"

The trainer answered quickly, "He was triple line bred. It's simply a matter of genetics."

The lineage of the horse was so inbred that he might have been beautiful to look at, and even quick to learn things, but genetics had dealt him an unstable mind. John nodded. There were some things that even he didn't have control over.

John learned a lot about his limitations but also learned that he didn't want to quit. He still had plenty of friends and family in and around Phoenix, so he decided to rent an apartment for a month, so that he, Susie, and the four kids could stay there. He got some sleeping bags, and they all slept on the apartment floor as if they were camping out. Ollie,

John's dad, was exasperated after seeing the kids sleeping on the floor and rented three beds and a dining room table for the family, so they wouldn't seem quite so transient.

Other training sessions were scheduled, so John extended his stay for another month, then another. He met Lloyd Kloppe, D.V.M., who wanted to hold a large clinic at his place south of Phoenix. When John arrived, he was surprised and delighted at what he found. Unlike his other scheduled dates, where he could count the number of riders and observers on two hands, this training clinic had about a hundred observers and twenty-five horses. John felt like he was in tall cotton. The horses were trained according to his methods, and the spectators were amazed at how the horses who had given their riders so many problems before were much more receptive to their riders. After that week, John was exhausted but satisfied. His life was finally going in the direction that he wanted it to. He loved making a difference to those horses and riders, and believed he'd finally found his place in the world.

He began traveling to local ranches throughout the West. He started out with a truck and camper shell with a two-horse trailer, and then found a big delivery-style van, like a windowless ice cream truck, which had a sliding door on the right-hand side. So John drove from clinic to clinic, all over the United States.

When John set up a clinic in Southern California, he and Susie decided to make a family vacation out of it as well, and take the kids to Disneyland. The kids piled into the back of a van and John drove the eight hours down the 60 freeway to Anaheim. As they neared the park, the kids were thrilled to see the sign for the "Happiest Place on Earth." The Lyonses couldn't afford to stay in any of the local motels, so John pulled into the parking lot of a nearby motel on Harbor Boulevard, just outside the gates of Disneyland. They stayed in the van so that they had enough money to buy tickets to the Magic Kingdom. Also, to keep expenses down, they ate bologna sandwiches and took showers at the local truck stops. Despite the unconventional vacation and the tight purse strings, somehow the family managed to laugh at most of it, and hang together.

Susie was tolerant of her odd lifestyle. She believed in what her husband was doing, so she supported his dreams even though many women would have put their foot down months previous. And she did see that he was making headway with this newfangled clinic stuff.

Word of mouth spread throughout the Southwest. People in California, Texas, and New Mexico would hear about him and agree to do a clinic. But despite the modest interest in his training, John was still in survival mode and didn't want anything to jeopardize the bookings. He'd had several bad experiences in which he had spent every last dime the family had to get to someone's place for a clinic. He'd arrive only to find out that no one had enrolled, and the posters he had sent a month prior would be sitting in a garage instead of posted at local tack stores.

Back at the ranch, Susie would work on creative marketing ideas. She came up with an advertising flyer, and started addressing them to ranch owners and equestrian center managers. Some would call to set up a clinic, but most did not want to make any guarantees to John. He and Susie struggled to think of ways to get the people to commit. Finally, they came up with a plan.

First, riders had to put down a deposit to be in the clinic. If the clinic host didn't produce at least two rider's' deposits, then the clinic would be canceled. This was the only way he thought people would follow through with their promise, and it would give him some peace of mind before showing up. At first he was nervous that he was asking too much of people. After all, having people send him a $50 to $250 deposit was no small thing, and he was afraid that no one would sign up at all.

To ease his anxiety, he decided to add a sales incentive for the hosts. He told them that if they filled the clinic to maximum capacity—fifteen riders—the host's horse would be worked for free. Finally, he decided to do something a little radical. Once someone contacted him to do a clinic, thirty days prior to the date, he cut off all contact with them—wouldn't call to re-confirm, wouldn't even answer his home phone when it rang—he was too afraid of cancellations. In the end, it usually worked out because even if he showed up and no one had committed to ride, he still put a clinic on for the host. Inevitably word of mouth garnered some spectators, too.

Whenever John got some money, he would send most of it home, then put the rest in the gas tank and head to the next clinic in the next town. The first year, most of John's clinics were just for the host. Then things started to grow, and he'd work with a pair of riders and their horses. Gradually more people signed up and sent in deposits, too. Relieved, John started holding regular dates, and slowly the clinics filled to capacity with participants and spectators.

In 1984, John got a call from a friend of a friend in Australia. Vic Dahl had contacted John to hold a couple of clinics down under. For John, it was the trip of a lifetime. He asked his dad if he would consider coming with him, and Ollie eagerly agreed. They packed for a three-week trip and got on a plane out of Denver. In Sydney, Vic met them at the gate, extended his hand, and shook John's warmly.

"Thanks for coming, mate. We got plenty to keep you busy."

John stayed three weeks in Australia, going to two different ranches for separate clinics. He stayed with the host of each clinic, who put him and his dad up in a spare room or in a bunkhouse. And while John was excited to be in a new country and see a new part of the world, he hardly had time to catch his breath, let alone sightsee. He worked from dawn till dusk each day, pausing only briefly for a quick midday break. In the time that he was there, he dropped nearly 25 pounds.

Australian horses such as the waler, Australian thoroughbred, and Australian stock horses are a lot more hot-blooded than the quarter horses and paints with which John normally worked. He learned a lot about how to get into the mind of a tough, hot horse. The intelligence of the horses

John at a clinic in Australia.

made them learn quickly, but John had to find ways in which to keep their lessons interesting. He also had to keep them focused, since they had such short fuses and would often spook and act up to end their lessons early.

When an exhausted John returned to America, he realized that he had a little more clout because of his trip abroad. He quickly updated his flyers to read "internationally known."

It was becoming more evident that John's talents were needed everywhere. Still thinking of different ways in which to reach more people and get the word out, John decided to contact national horse magazines. He'd read about a lot of training methods in magazines that were not only dangerous and borderline cruel, but they also didn't seem that effective in the long run.

He worked with Susie to get an article together on one simple training topic. After deciding on the topic—how to cross a creek—they sat up night after night, writing out notes on yellow ledger pads and then typing

them, double spaced, on the office Selectric. He even had Susie take some photos at their nearby stream and used a couple of their horses to demonstrate the methods step-by-step. When it was complete, John got a big manila envelope, put the whole package together, and mailed it away to a national horse magazine. About six weeks later, he got a reply from the magazine. He ripped the envelope open eagerly but found his manuscript returned, along with the photos.

"They rejected the manuscript because it wasn't dramatic enough. I guess they're looking for us to show a wreck," John told Susie disappointedly. He'd chosen quiet horses and had selected a method where the horse approached and successfully crossed the water trouble-free. John thought that showing horses doing their job without a fuss was a good thing, but the magazine felt there wasn't enough of a fight to be interesting.

Undeterred, he sent the manuscript to another horse magazine. This time, he got a reply back in just a few weeks. It was a one-page letter. They were accepting the article for publication.

As John's name started cropping up in local newspaper and magazine features, he decided it would be good to support the magazines with ads so that people could find out how to reach him for more clinics.

John's path crossed with Sharon Jordan-McCreary's, a unique young woman with a gift for writing. She had grown up in Alaska in a town so remote that she had never met another female other than her mother during her childhood. She had never known another girl her age for a good portion of her life. John met her at a clinic in Phoenix, and she decided to visit John in Colorado.

"John, I'd really like to write some articles about your training methods. I know I'll be able to get you in magazines all the time."

Her talent for putting words to paper turned out to be a boon for John. She crafted two articles, which both got published back to back and helped spread the word.

John's clinics continued to grow steadily. Attendance was up tremendously, and suddenly there were more horses than he could train in one day. He had gained a reputation for being able to fix complicated problem horses. They were either completely unbroken, or they had severe behavioral problems. He was not only solving simple problems but also working with a lot of horses who were dangerous for their riders. Because he worked so hard on each and every horse, his schedule of being on the road was beginning to wear on him. He found himself in the beginning stages of burnout.

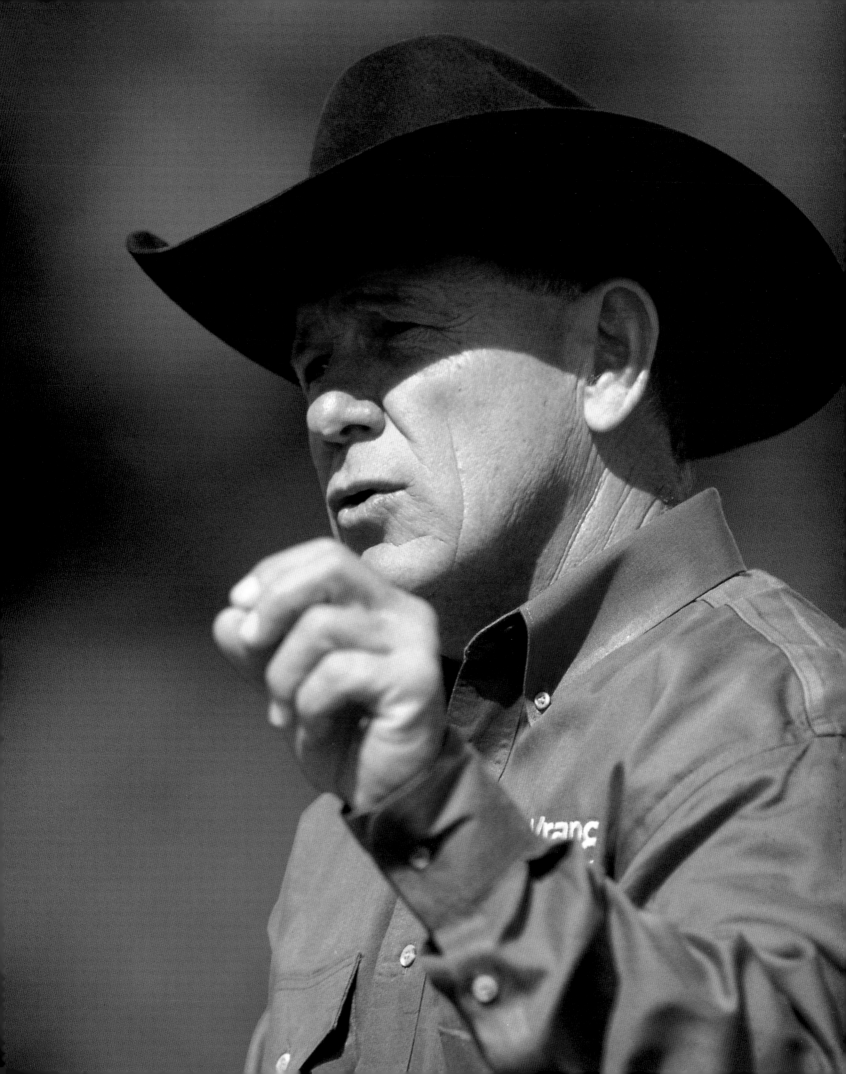

He recalled the first clinic that he had attended, and remembered the clinician was short-tempered with some of the horses, and a little rude to the people who attended. Questions were not handled with tact or courtesy. John kept this in mind when he was doing his clinics, but he realized that he was on his way to behaving similarly if he kept up the grueling pace. He talked it over with Susie.

"Maybe you should set a limit. Like see what the maximum number of clinics you want to hold in one calendar year, and once those are all full, that will be it."

John thought about it and agreed. He needed to set boundaries, otherwise he would be forever driving here and there to private farms and small ranches, giving clinics too frequently, to only a handful of people. He needed to reduce the traveling, yet still have the same amount of participants attending overall. Now with a new goal in mind, he thought about

82

morphing his clinics into something else. This became the constant thought in the forefront of his mind. Each year during the mid-eighties as the clinics grew in size, he tried to schedule fewer stops.

John met many people along the way during his clinics. One major influence who helped him understand how to handle both horses and people was Doug Householder, Ph.D., whom John had met while holding a clinic at Texas A&M. Doug, an extension horse specialist at the university and a member of the equine science section in the Department of Animal Science, was also a carded judge and had long been regarded as one of the most knowledgeable individuals in the horse industry.

Doug came and rode his horses with John during that clinic, and together they discussed training philosophy and technique. They worked until one o'clock every morning, developing different solutions to training problems and schooling methods. John learned even more about equine behavior and body language. They experimented with new ideas. After the clinic, John met Doug for dinner. Doug presented John with a small microphone from Radio Shack and speakers. "Here, John. With all the talking you're going to be doing in the future, you're going to be needing this."

In the winter of 1986, John had a clinic scheduled in Las Vegas. Temperatures usually dipped into the low 20s in Clark County at night and barely broke 40 degrees during the day. It was particularly gray and windy through the Vegas valley when John rolled into town. John was used to changeable climates, but that day looked a little different. He went to the facility where the clinic was being held. They had a round pen set up and bleachers for the spectators. More than a dozen horses were scheduled for the weekend, and John knew he had his work cut out for him in the cold.

The spectators filed into the bleachers and huddled under blankets or were bundled up in down jackets and woolly mittens. About an hour into the clinic, John noticed the skies blacken. Instead of rain, snowflakes started to fall on the desert, and the wind whipped through the pen. John was using the Radio Shack microphone, but his voice was inaudible, even with the small speakers. John could barely make out the people seated on the freezing metal bleachers. He was shivering under his jacket, and he knew that the spectators were also freezing and straining to hear him as well. Yet no one left the bleachers. They were transfixed by the information they'd been receiving that morning.

John peered into the audience and had a realization as he looked into their expectant faces. He thought, *You know, I can train only so many horses, but I can talk to a lot of people. And the number of people that I can talk to at the same time is unlimited.* He smiled at their fortitude. He'd had an epiphany.

That night, as he warmed up in the hotel room, he told Susie what had been going through his mind. "This new style of clinic—we could hold it indoors, too! That way we won't be at the mercy of the weather."

"Spectators will be able to hear you better indoors, too. You won't have to yell, and most places have pretty good sound systems."

They talked into the night excitedly about how they would make a new learning experience designed for the observer, rather than just for the participant. When he returned home, they continued to formulate the idea and develop more details. John wanted to figure out ways in which to market this idea to a variety of horse lovers.

They got a few ideas from Ken and Martha Moore, a couple from southern Texas who told them how to use a timeline for their new business. Susie came up with the concept of turning the clinic into a true event.

"Why not schedule it over several days, and we can entertain as well as educate!" she exclaimed. No one else was doing that in the industry. Susie developed a newsletter to do small mailings. She wanted it to list all the fun things that they were planning for the upcoming "super clinics." Besides the horse training, they wanted participants to be able to meet and interact with each other. Susie thought that social gatherings during the clinic such as a welcome barbecue dinner, a pancake breakfast, and a dance on Saturday night would allow clinic goers a memorable time.

The only problem was that John felt the events could no longer be called clinics. He didn't want them to be confused by the customary ones that he was doing—he wanted to ensure that people could plan vacations around their week with him. But what to call them? He started with his bookshelf and looked up the definition of various terms in the dictionary. The first one he thought about was "*seminar*" but noted that it emphasized a gathering of people who are getting together to listen to one or two speakers regarding a particular subject. He cross-referenced clinic for other words that might be synonymous. The word symposium cropped up. John flipped to the dictionary and felt it was ideal: a group of individuals meeting socially to share ideas and eat and drink. He told Susie excitedly, "We're going to call them symposiums. John Lyons Symposiums."

Susie thought of other tips and fun activities to put in the newsletter, then it was down to the copy store and the post office. They mailed out the newsletters by the dozens—an update for all the clinic hosts and

John's second symposium in Pomona, California.

attendees from the past. They hoped they were on the way to changing the way people thought about their relationship with horses.

They really wanted to make an impression on the horse industry. John's clinics had been pulling in about one hundred spectators and participants a day. "I bet we could get five hundred people at our symposiums," John told Susie. "Let's think big. We should make a big splash the first time out." They came up with a weekend ticket for $48.50. Attendees would receive a pancake breakfast, a barbecue dinner, Sunday morning church service, and even a souvenir T-shirt. It couldn't miss!

John scheduled the first symposium to be held in February of 1988 at the Earl Warren show grounds, in Santa Barbara, ten months away. While they had advertised only in local horse papers before, he made the decision to advertise nationally.

"You'll need some support from local businesses," said Susie. "You could do a mini–trade fair. Get local merchants to bring their stuff to the fairgrounds." So they went to Santa Barbara early. John combed the area, from Montecito to Goleta, and tried to get businesses to take booth space for $250. This would offset the costs of paying for the entire grounds. John would provide the drapes and tables for each booth, so all they had to do was show up with product in hand. It was hard to think that John was going from simple horse training to trade show management, but he told Susie, "I really think it will be a huge success if we do it up big."

John rented a tent since the arena wasn't enclosed. He also hired a band.

Only 125 people showed up for the first symposium. He probably didn't even need his microphone in the tent, since he was talking to the same number of people he had at his clinics. The event was scheduled for the entire weekend. On Saturday night, they had scheduled a dance, but other than John and Susie, there was only one other couple on the dance floor.

John lost about $30,000 on Santa Barbara, and was not only thoroughly depressed that the idea wasn't well received, he also was distraught about the money. But not to be daunted, he forged ahead to the next scheduled symposium at the Los Angeles County Fairgrounds, in Pomona. Again, John made the rounds on the miles of L.A. freeways, going to every tack store in the area. He posted flyers at the Broken Horn Saddlery and at Foothill Feed. He sent out newsletters to every address he could find. He sat in crawling traffic on freeway after freeway, trying to contact as many people as possible.

This time he was rewarded for his efforts. Nearly 450 showed up at Pomona.

Fairground personnel set up the symposium in one of the large brick buildings, normally reserved for flower and garden shows. John and Susie, with the kids, set up their round pen, and they looked for a place to set up their speakers. Their only option was to duct tape them directly to the round pen. People began to file in eagerly the first morning and took their places in chairs around the pen.

John arrived and entered the arena. "I'd like to welcome you to a new experience: a symposium," he began. His voice echoed and bounced off the brick walls, feeding back with a squeal. His crew ran over to adjust the volume. "I'd like to begin with—" again the sound reverberated and continued to do so throughout the entire clinic. At certain points, John could barely make out his own words, so he tried his best to talk loudly off the microphone. Toward the end, he was hoarse from shouting, but the symposium was a success.

Next came Arizona, then Texas. Each town they went to, they had to sell themselves to local tack stores, western stores, farm and feed shops, anyplace where a horse person might come into contact with him. The stress, coupled with the uncertainty, the grueling travel schedule, and the hard work took its toll on Susie. When they were in Texas, she had a breakdown. She couldn't take the lifestyle on the road anymore.

John knew he was asking too much of Susie, so he hired Linda Tate, a woman with strong administrative skills, to help take up the slack. She immediately helped take the pressure off the organization. Shortly after, John hired John Sparks as the Road Manager. Both hit the road with John and helped with the preparation and execution of each symposium. That first year, however, was financially atrocious. Travel costs, staffing salaries, rental of equipment and event halls had not proved to be profitable. He ended the season more than $90,000 in the hole.

Still, John felt that the symposiums would catch on eventually, and that if he could just find a way to stick it out financially, he would be making money instead of losing it. While in Texas, he met George Myers out in Kingsville. George was a wealthy, successful businessman. John spent a week at his home and redefined what would make the symposiums not only profitable but also more meaningful.

"I'm going to get partners, George, I've got to. I'll get some money together, and I can start in the Pacific Northwest this time."

After a week of listening to John's ruminations, George had had it. "Look, John, I'm not going to be your partner. I really don't want to do that," he huffed. He reached into his office desk drawer and pulled out his ledger book, scribbled, then tore off the paper. "Here. Take this. It's a check for $20,000. Consider it a loan."

With that, John headed back to Colorado. He was back in business. He had scheduled sixteen symposiums for that year, 1989, and began to plan in earnest for his second year of symposiums. He knew he had to cut costs and keep his overhead down to make that start-up money last. He didn't hire anyone for that year, relying on only the staff that he currently had. He asked people to volunteer helping out with things such as setting up the booth and running the cash register, in exchange for a free ticket to the show. His thriftiness paid off because after the sixteen symposiums were complete, he was nearly out of debt.

John paid George back the $20,000 a year later.

George's accountant called John upon receiving his check. "You know, Mr. Lyons, George couldn't believe that he got your check. This is the first time he's ever been paid back on a loan on time."

can come up. I kind of feel like they're at a disadvantage because they don't get to practice—they don't get the opportunity to make and correct their mistakes—except on a much larger scale. In a way, I'm grateful for all the years of experience that I now have. I've been known to make people laugh at a situation instead of being at a loss for words when training doesn't always go as planned. You gotta know what to do when a wreck happens, and when in front of people, you need to know how to handle their emotions (and your own) at the same time.

Chapter

5

WORKING IN THE ROUND

Something happened when John touched a horse.

In handling the equine, he could also make other connections on several different levels. Physically, he was able to make contact with them, but in his gentle working and training sessions, his methods also touched their spirit. He had a gift in joining the horse's mind, body, and character with his own, resulting in a harmonious partnership between human and horse.

It was 1979 and John was looking for inspiration to help him hone his horse training skills. He searched continuously to improve his knowledge base—to find a way in which he could reach more horses effectively and affect more equestrians positively. He bounced ideas off other respected horsemen, he voraciously read a host of books on training and philosophy, and he practiced, practiced, practiced.

That year he attended a local training clinic given by a pretty well-known horseman. He looked forward to being inspired by a trainer with new ideas and insights. What he found, however, was thoroughly disappointing. First, John saw that the trainer was not concerned for anyone's safety—including his own. Second, John quickly noticed that the trainer had the presence of a man who had been working without joy, and was well past the stage of job burnout. He was short-tempered with some of the horses, and tactless with a few attendees.

Still, John gleaned some important lessons from that clinic. He knew that he got more joy and pride from working with horses than from any other career he had been in or could be in. He knew that he had the talent to take his skills to the next level. And as he was standing with the rest of the attendees, he realized that people—lots of them—had a great desire and commitment to learn. He also learned that it was really important to always put safety first—for both horse and handler. Finally, he found some basic training techniques that would be perfect for his own program.

The horseman worked with horses and people in a small round pen. The rails extended up about 5 feet, and the pen was probably 40 feet in diameter. John was fascinated at how much potential a pen with no corners could have for working a loose horse. The advantages were obvious to John right away. If he was working a horse from the ground in a square pen, the horse might get stuck in one of the corners. He'd seen the concept in Kentucky, where large green pastures surrounded by tidy post-and-rail fencing often had rounded corners so that one horse couldn't trap another. Horses who panicked in their effort to get away from a trainer often tried the fence more—either by going over it or running through it, so there was a safety advantage to a completely round pen.

Upon returning to the ranch, John began to fashion his own round pen. After selecting a level part of the ranch, he gathered together some wooden boards and railroad ties. He set the railroad ties into the ground as posts, then placed the boards on the ties. He stood back and nodded his head, pleased with the first result.

Once he put it to use, John quickly discovered other benefits of working in the round pen. He found that by observing the horse's body language and then using those visual cues to help control the horse, a round pen actually stimulated the horse's mind. Local horsemen came by and watched as John trained a horse in his new pen.

"Can't you just direct him by putting him on a longe line?" asked one neighbor.

"Well, I'm not looking at telling him what I want. When I do it this way, I'm not giving the horse the answer," replied John, as he allowed a big-boned gelding to trot the parameter. "I could have him on a rope and then pull him around to trot in the other direction, but I want him to figure it out. Watch." John stepped in the direction of the horse's shoulder and, using body language, gave him a cue to stop. The horse abruptly halted. Then John cued the horse again with his posture, and the horse pivoted on his hind end, then jogged in the other direction. "See that? I

want him to change directions, but I'm not forcing him. He's gotta figure out what I want from him."

The neighbor leaned over the fence. "I still don't understand."

John spoke as he continued to have the horse stop and change directions. "He's figuring out that he's doing what I want without me forcing him to do it. When I first started, this horse tried a lot of different options. He tried to go faster, tried darting past me, tried to stop and turn away from me. Then, all of a sudden, he stumbled onto the option that I wanted." Again, John shifted his body toward the horse's front end and the gelding whirled around and jogged in the other direction.

"How does he know he's doing what you want?" the man said.

"I keep putting the pressure on him, keep after him, kinda like asking him a question. The minute he gives me the right answer, I back off and release the pressure immediately. Since he's the one that's figuring it out,

MASTERING THE ART OF HORSEMANSHIP

he's much more confident with his choices and, he's focused on me, rather than himself. He came up with the idea, he knows ten things that don't work, and one that does, and realizes it is easier to do what I want rather than not."

And so it went with every horse John began to work in the round pen. He found that there was a major advantage to working a horse loose and allowing him time to come up with the correct "answer" on his own. But there were other advantages to the round pen, as well. Shortly after he first started having success with horses in the round pen, John began working with a fractious colt who didn't respect his owner's space. The colt ran over the top of him whenever his owner led him around. Even worse, the colt was very spooky; occasionally when he was leading like a well-mannered horse, he would become startled and leap into his owner's side. When John began to work with this colt in the round pen, he found that since he wasn't connected to the colt by way of saddle, bridle, or lead rope, it was safer for him. The lessons inspired confidence, not fear, so it took a lot of pressure off the horse. And John was able to establish control and communicate without having to actually physically touch the horse.

With every success John had in the round pen, he would excitedly chronicle his efforts. He made it known that this was a remarkable way to get rid of bad habits and establish correct ones. One woman whose ten-year-old gelding had a plethora of bad habits—he refused to trailer load, didn't like his feet handled, was head-shy—brought her horse over to see John. "He just doesn't respect me. I have got to get his respect and trust. Can you help us?"

John looked at both of them, then thought for a moment before speaking. "Well, respect and trust—you can't demand those things. I can't make you respect me, nor can I make you trust me. Let's say you're a horse. I can't beat you enough for you to respect or trust me." John went on to explain that respect and trust were things that anyone could give, but never something that they could demand.

"Believe it or not, respect is a byproduct of control," John began as he took the horse's lead rope from the woman. "Let me give you a scenario. Was there ever a guy in school who just adored you? A guy who thought you were the sweetest thing and was like a puppy at your feet?"

She nodded.

John continued, "Now this Mr. Nice Guy was just an absolute pushover, wasn't he? He saw whatever movie you wanted, and took you to dinner wherever you fancied. He just didn't care, as long as he was hanging out with you. And what did you do after a while?"

In John's Words

There is one thing that seems to be the foundation for everything else in horse training, and you should try to establish with the horse no matter what type of rider you are or what level you ride. You can establish it in those first moments in the round pen—and that's control. Now control isn't a bad word. Control keeps a little kid from dashing out in front of a car and getting killed. Control keeps a horse from running through fences and getting both horse and rider killed. So control is not a freakish type of restriction, but rather a safety measure. Now a lot of times, equine fears are a major blockage to control. To let you have control, work him in a loose and safe environment—like a round pen—which not only allows the horse to concentrate solely on you but also is a secure area where the horse and you are safe.

Trust is a byproduct of control without pain. If I can control a horse, yet not hurt him while doing so, then he will recognize that he can be around me. I can get him to do things, and he'll know that I'm not going to cause pain to get him to do them. The longer I can control him, the more he learns he can trust me. If I'm just standing in a round pen, he never has to trust me. I have to control him and be working with him without pain or coercion in order to develop that trust. It's a natural equation.

"I broke up with him," she replied sheepishly.

"That's right. You wanted someone with opinions and a mind of his own. You didn't want some dog at your feet. Now think of your ideal relationship. You'd trade off on things you both wanted to do, places that you wanted to go. There was compromise. It was like you both had moderate control over where the relationship was going, and both of you brought something to the relationship.

"You see, it's kind of the same way with a horse. We can feed him carrots, let him run over the top of us, step on us, and possibly hurt us. We may allow him to do this because we think loving him will change his behavior, but he'll never respect us. But if I begin controlling him in just a few areas, then he must learn to deal with me."

As an example, John walked into the pen with her young colt, but just stood there. The horse looked at him but ignored his presence. "See? He never has to deal with the question 'Does he trust me?' I'm just in the pen. But watch."

John's body language took on a new direction. He began to ask the colt to trot to the left by stepping towards his rear end. The colt had to acknowledge John's presence, that he was alive and taking up space, and react to it. However, the colt had several choices—some radical, others simple. He could have tried to jump the fence or go in the other direction. He could have stopped and stood perfectly still. Even more radical, he could have charged John aggressively, bit him, or kicked out. When the horse realized that John was asking him to do something, such as go to the left, he began to recognize that he was performing a task, and the embers of control were ignited.

"You have to understand that it's more than just acknowledging my presence. Once I can control him, he'll start to acknowledge that I'm alive and should be reckoned with. After that, respect and trust begins."

John's philosophy about training was simple: Control without pain equals respect and trust. And when he added up those three qualities, the sum was equal to a relationship. John believed this was a universal quality to be applied to any two individuals, whether husband and wife, boss and coworker, or family members.

Attaining respect and trust by using the round pen for control was made easier because John wasn't touching or attached to the horse in any way. This was especially powerful when he worked with horses who were truly fearful of humans. He was able to get frightened horses to respond to his actions, and learn how to respond correctly and calmly, and be con-

It's important that we teach a horse to answer the way we want. For example, if I ask you the question "Will you give me $10,000?" I am looking for the answer "yes," yet there are three answers you could give me: yes, no, and maybe. Most likely, your answer is no, but your answer isn't wrong to you. In your perception, you gave me the right answer. Is it the answer I want? No...

But how about this: "What if I were to give you $10,000?" Your answer would be yes. So if I want you to answer yes, it's important that I ask the right question. As teachers of the horse, we want to blame the horse's attitude; the horse isn't doing it correctly, he isn't giving me the right answer. The problem is I'm teaching the subject wrong! An equine student only learns what I teach.

trolled before he ever actually placed a hand on the animal. This was crucial for horses who had been neglected, abused, or were once wild.

John believed that horse training is basically nothing more than a series of asking questions. He asks the horse a question, which is simply "Will you do this?" The "this" could be any of a multitude of tasks. For any question he asks, John could receive one of three answers: yes, no, or let me think about it. The answers that John really didn't want to deal with were the latter two.

As the trainer, or the teacher, John was committed to being responsible for what his "student" learned. He knew that many people blamed the student, saying that the horse's attitude was poor, or that he was stubborn, obstinate, or stupid. Yet John knew that it had nothing to do with the horse and everything to do with his trainer. John broke his training down so that the question he asked of a horse was so unbelievably simple that he automatically said yes, as was the case of the fractious colt whom he wanted to go left. John approached him in such a way that it was incredibly easy for the colt to do so. Then he asked the horse to change direction, and the horse once again answered yes by complying. Within about twenty minutes, John was able to establish more than twenty different opportunities for questions to be answered. Pretty soon, when John asked the horse something new, the horse would comply quickly and easily. The obedience was something that became so strong that the horse said yes before he could say no. John got the horse in the habit of compliance, and focused on getting him to answer with at least the smallest try, so that the habits of correct behavior would be established. It was as though the horse was thinking *"Perhaps I can't do everything you ask, but for now, this one's easy."*

In the round pen, John found the environment to be somewhat of a safe haven for a horse. After studying how many horses moved and reacted to their space in the corral, John decided to refine and further craft it.

John found that the safety of the materials and design were of utmost importance to both horse and rider. When he first started doing clinics, John would just borrow fence or stock panels that were locally available. Once, when he was in Houston, he was working a really nice reining and cutting horse who belonged to Martha Moore. The fence that he'd borrowed was designed with a flat piece of metal with a 90-degree bend in the other direction as the center support bar. This makeshift panel had a hole cut in it where a pipe was slid through and spot-welded.

*Working in the
round pen.*

He loped the horse around the circumference of the pen. Suddenly the
horse took a misstep and hit his front knee on the edge of the metal. The
sharp edge sliced the knee right open in a huge gash. The horse could
have been crippled for life. John decided that he'd had enough of making
do with inadequate materials. He'd design his own panel.

The size was an important consideration. If the round pen was 100
feet in diameter, he wasn't able to establish control effectively. It acted like
a huge arena instead of an area for training. A horse in a pen of that size
could easily get to the far end and be away from John's influence. But 60
feet in diameter—that was ideal. It was large enough so that a horse
loping around the rail would be in his own safety zone but could still be
controlled by the trainer. Even better, John found that the circle size didn't
put undue stress on a horse's tendons and lower legs. John quickly found
out that 40 feet was way too close for comfort when a horse once spun

around and kicked out toward the center, missing him by only a couple of feet. Plus, he found that in a small pen he was always on top of the horse, which crowded the horse and made him more prone to stopping, locking up, wanting to strike out in defense or panic and jump over the rails. With a pen larger than 40 feet, John found that horses didn't want to leap out of the corral as often, and in fact they respected the boundaries of the rails better. They felt more comfortable when there was enough room to move around and make their own decisions.

John also was critical about the materials his round pens were made of—especially after that horse's injury—and spent a great deal of time engineering the perfect design. He traveled to other ranches and training facilities and saw what they had.

There was a "bullpen" style that he saw throughout the West. These were made of solid wooden walls, up to 6 feet in height, that looked like a tiny bullfighting arena. With tall paneled walls, the horse was less likely to think about going over the fence. The panels, often made of plywood, kept the horse from being distracted by outside events, since he wouldn't be able to see anything on the other side. But John found that there were a lot of pens with the wall slanting outward from the ground. These types of pens John found to be completely unsuitable for working or riding horses. The first time he rode in a slanted bullpen, he remarked to the barn manager, "Man, this is strange. I keep looking at the wall when I'm about three feet away and thinking that's how far I am from it. But it's a total optical illusion. Plus, this horse here has scrambled along the side of the walls just because of how he perceives the fence."

The owner said, "We got some riders who like to work their horses in here because they don't bump their legs along the fence, since it slants out."

"Well, that's just crazy. Can't they just ride in a regular pen and not hug the wall so closely? Plus, it's really hot in here. This design works like one of those face reflectors that people use for suntans. I think by the end of a schooling session, these riders would be fried."

The owner laughed. "Yep, I hear you. Have any suggestions for a better design?"

"I'm working on it," John replied.

So John went to the drawing board. He thought about the elements of a perfect training ring. While he could see how tall wooden panels cut out distractions, he didn't buy it, since riders and trainers don't work in a sterile environment. There are plenty of distractions wherever people ride, from the hubbub of the show grounds, to the natural flora and fauna of the

trails. He could understand that having the horse free from distractions forced the horse to focus on the handler. But the disadvantage is that he wouldn't have the choice to look at him. So he decided that he would build his pen of pipe rails, and the panels would be easily portable.

John learned a really hard lesson about pipe rails one weekend—one that would change how he designed his pens. On the ranch there were cattle gates all over the place, including in front of each stall in the barn. John liked the fact that he could open the gates, drive a tractor into the stall, clean it out, and drive to the next. The gates had pipes that were very close together toward the bottom. They had seemed to work okay until one weekend, when John scheduled all the horses to be seen by the vet for their deworming.

John gathered up the mares, stallions, and geldings and brought them into the barn. The alleyway to the barn was 24 by 80 feet wide, and

one of the older studs, Ben Lo, began to get agitated by another stallion down the barn. During the night, the agitation escalated, and Ben Lo was pawing at the front gate, and stuck his foot through the narrow bars of the panel. When he tried to yank his leg back out, it became stuck and he panicked. The bars were too close together and his leg broke in the gate. John found Ben Lo that morning when the vet arrived, but it was too late. The old stud had to be put down. A disconsolate John ripped out the pipes that were close together.

He had learned a lesson from this tragedy. When John designed his sectional round pen panels, he made sure that if any horse got his leg between the bars, he would still be able to get it back out. Plus, there was another good reason for changing the placement of the bars that John found was an added bonus. People at his clinics would be able to see into the pen—even those who sat in folding chairs right next to the fence. His

center support braces, made of the same material as the horizontal bars, were rounded off so that they wouldn't cut anyone working in the pen. His panels were fully square, so that a horse's leg couldn't get caught where two sections connect with each other. The bottom rail of each panel was high enough off the ground so that a horse would not get a foot caught easily as in other pens.

His sectional panels completed, John took the round pen on the road with him. And sure enough, it worked. In fact, people responded so well to his new panel that he began to see companies copying his design. John didn't mind that they were using all his "research and development" for their panels—it just meant that problems would be averted.

The more that round pens came into vogue, the more that trainers, and then regular horsemen and women, started using them. Some trainers believed that all a horse needs is to be worked in a round pen. They stuck old campaigners, youngsters, you name it, into the enclosure and sent them around. But John was a firm believer that "if it ain't broke, don't fix it."

Never was this more apparent than when John was giving a clinic to about fifteen people. One of the observers had a well-schooled show horse. He was well mannered in the cross-ties, and he didn't have any problems with being saddled, groomed, clipped, bathed, or trailered. He was a perfect gentleman on the ground. But the owner really wanted him to be worked in the round pen like the other horses John was working with.

"John, I want you to work him in the round pen."

"He really doesn't need it though."

"Please, John. I'd really like to see how he works for you."

John reluctantly agreed and walked the horse over to the pen, which John knew was small and a bit on the makeshift side. John explained to her that, at best, the round pen was pretty unsafe with its 4-1/2 foot panels. He set the horse loose in the pen, then turned to close the gate. The horse dashed off, and halfway around the pen, ran right into the fence, slashing his legs to pieces. John hadn't even had time to turn back around.

The owner ran up to him and screamed, "What did you do to my horse?"

"Lady, I haven't even started working with him yet. I just walked him into the pen and then he ran into the fence." He caught the horse and had him stand still until the vet came to stitch him up, all the while trying to explain to the owner that she was the one who insisted he be worked in the pen. Because of an unnecessary mishap, a nice, calm horse, was laid up for weeks.

In John's Words

Any time you work with a horse, it's a risk. That risk should be made as minimal as possible.

The round pen is not a cure-all. It won't fix everything. It's no different from taking a horse and teaching him to back up on a lead rope. That will teach a horse to work on his attitude just as much as chasing him around in a round pen. So it's just a tool, not a necessity for all horses. Sometimes it's safer for the rider or the handler to work the horse in a round pen, and sometimes it's not.

Chapter

6

ABOUT *DREAM*

It was probably only a year or two before John developed his round pen that he started spending a lot of time on the road with his clinics and Dream came into his life. When the big bay five-year-old American quarter horse crossed John's path in 1982, John knew that it wasn't just chance that they met.

Sometimes it seems there is a greater plan at work. That was the case with Dream and John. While John had been experiencing success at his early clinics, he knew there was room to grow and more to learn when it came to training. Perhaps what he needed most was a challenge.

It seemed more and more that whenever people saw John's amazing Appaloosa stallion, Zip, they were a little flippant about the extent of the horse's training. Most thought that Zip was an extraordinary example of a finely tuned horse—some even thought he was a total freak of nature. Observers and skeptics refused to believe that Zip's performance and behavior were a result of John's patient training methods.

Some wanted to think that the horse was unique from all other studs. Despite being a stallion, Zip rarely acted like one. Many scoffed, saying that he must have been really easy to train, although John knew what painstaking effort had gone into making Zip the partner he was. But because critics were loud about how simple it must have been to work

John and Dream
in 1985.

with a horse like Zip and that John should put his methods to a real test, John decided that he would hand select one of the most badly behaved stallions he could find and retrain him.

John didn't have to search very far. He found what he was looking for only 14 miles north in the area called Silt Mesa, Colorado. His name was South Dakota Dream, a registered American quarter horse. The young bay stud had been broken to saddle and had been ridden a scant handful of times. Even though the horse had some really bad habits and was dangerous, he was being bred regularly at the cost of $500 per breeding. John ended up trading seven horses for Dream so that the total value for him was $20,000—the amount his owners would have made on him as a stud for one year.

The breeders took the seven horses with the understanding that they still had the opportunity to use Dream as a stud for the remainder of that season. They sold a few of the Lyons' horses for about $22,000, so they were pretty satisfied with their deal. And John got his first real super-problem horse.

Dream was a challenging animal—one of the toughest horses John had come across. He had several behavioral issues that made him dangerous. One was biting, a habit that John took seriously. Dream didn't just lash out with his teeth because he was agitated. Dream learned early on that he could bite his handlers when they'd asked too much of him or if he'd had enough of a situation. Fortunately, he wasn't the type of stud who would stand his ground, biting repeatedly, as that type often has the dubious reputation of rearing and striking out at handlers, too. No, Dream was a bit more calculated than that. He would clamp down on his handler with his teeth, then release his hold and bolt off at a run.

Several people were the unfortunate recipients of Dream's nasty bites. When he was younger, Dream attacked a young groom, and his former handlers had to crack a 2" x 4" over his head to get the stud to release the man. At the time that John bought him, no one would go into the stall with him. If his stall was being cleaned, the groom would make sure that the horse was herded outside into his run before slamming the door behind him. He would then muck out the stall, replace the bedding, slip out quietly, and then open the door to let Dream charge back in.

Breeding also had to be carefully orchestrated. The big stallion would stand in his stall with the top of his Dutch door opened and would have a halter and rope snapped on him. His groom would then pull open the bottom half of the door and Dream would scream and dash down the stable aisle in search of the mare, eyes blazing. There was no chance for quiet introductions—Dream would mount the mare and forcefully copulate, then when he was finished and a little more docile, the groom would yank him by the halter back into the stall.

The breeders told dozens of stories about Dream's bad behavior— and they'd handled many stallions who had covered hundreds of mares. When he was two years old, Dream was a handsome young colt and his breeder wanted to show him at halter. Dream presented a gorgeous picture at halter, but the breeder knew he had his hands full with the youngster. The stable workers used to place bets on which handler could hold onto him the longest while they longed him. Dream developed the habit of loping around on the longe line in a nice circle; when he decided he'd had enough, he'd leave by galloping away at full charge. The handler would desperately try to hang on. The horse was always wearing a stud chain, snapped to the outer ring of his halter and over the noseband to the inside halter ring, to try to keep him from bolting. But because of Dream's constant pulling against the handler, by the time he was three, the chain destroyed a good deal of cartilage on the bridge of his nose.

John took the stud to his ranch and put him in his barn. It took many months before the horse stopped being a nightmare and began to reflect his dreamy name. He was a sea of complexities, and John knew he had a major challenge ahead. John worked with him diligently for a couple months before he even allowed the horse to return to the breeder to start covering their first mares. He spent hours rubbing his nose and face so much that the last thing Dream wanted to do was put his nose—or his mouth—near a human body. John would ride him a little each day, but not so much that he tried the horse's patience. He knew he had to work at an extra slow pace to gain the horse's confidence and keep within Dream's tolerance threshold. With Dream being quite aware of how much more powerful he was than humans were, John was careful about the way he was reintroducing the concept of *trainer* to the horse.

When it came time to temporarily return Dream to his previous owners for the breeding season, the horse had made incredible progress. The breeders were amazed at the difference when Dream unloaded easily and without drama from the trailer. They stood with their mouths open when John handed the lead rope to a groom and Dream calmly and quietly followed behind, without any stud chain under his lip or over his nose. He was like a different horse!

But John's work was far from over. It took several months of short but frequent schooling sessions to get Dream to the point where he was trustworthy. John wanted to make sure that Dream would never be aggressive toward mares or humans again, so he devised a plan to break him of his bad habit using equine logic.

John tackled this when he decided to breed a couple of his mares to the stud himself. When the first mare went into season, John knew it was time to test his training. He led Dream out of his stall, down the aisleway, and then turned right, out of the barn. The mare was tied a few yards away. She was tied to the breeding post and Scotch hobbled, so she wouldn't be able to kick out at him with any velocity. When John led Dream toward the mare, the stud reacted by tearing the lead rope from John's hands and whirling past him toward the hobbled mare. He attacked her much like he had every other mare in his past.

John then decided to select a mare who wasn't in heat and quickly tied her up, but this time without the hobbles. He then retrieved a long rope from the tack shed and secured it to a ring outside the barn door. He carefully measured the rope as he tied it so that it would reach just the back of her—almost to her tail—but not quite. John led Dream out of the barn, quickly reached down and picked up the rope, then snapped it to his halter. Dream jerked away from John, just as he did the time before and made his customary rush around the corner to the waiting mare. Just as he tried to mount the mare, the rope he was tethered to yanked him shy of his goal. And the surprised mare, who was not in season, angrily kicked back at the confused stallion, repeatedly raining blows against his chest and barrel. A bewildered Dream beat a hasty retreat back into the barn. After that, he learned quickly that patience was a virtue.

Dream wasn't born with a cruel streak, nor was he different from many stallions around the world. Stallions are indeed unique from mares and geldings, and because of this, many people become afraid of them, and rightly so. A stallion by nature is supposed to fight harder against his opponent because it is often another horse who is trying to steal his mares. He is supposed to protect his mares and is genetically predisposed to fight for them.

Trainers can handle most breeding stallions so that they don't pose any danger to the people around them. Some of these handlers accomplish this by picking on the horse, attempting to overcome the stallion. They use a lip chain over the sensitive gum line of the animal to lead him around. They whip and beat the horse to make him behave, causing most studs to back down. These horses know they ultimately cannot win a fight.

There are, however, studs who refuse to back down. No matter how much they are beaten, they will not give in. The harder they get punished to give up control, the more they fight back. John once saw a brutal example of this in Dream when he and Susie were returning to the ranch after a day spent in town.

Dream was in the pasture with some mares on the ranch property, while down the road there was a pasture that held a few geldings, more mares, and three young stud colts of John's. During the time that John and Susie were absent, Dream had found a way to escape from his original pasture, taking his mares with him. He herded them down the road until they stood in the lower pasture with the other horses. John and Susie drove closer, and John could see that

In John's Words

A nervous handler might enter a stud's stall armed with a pitchfork or a harsh, angry voice commanding him to back away, even if the horse has not lashed out or bitten anyone. When a handler gets aggressive very quickly, wanting to get that halter on the stud without problems, he may lace a chain over the horse's nose to lead the horse out of his stall. Even if the stallion is well behaved, if he does something, such as walking too quickly, or possibly glancing away from the handler, that person will give a sharp yank on the chain. The horse gets hurt and pretty soon, whenever he hears that stall door open, he knows that someone will be yelling and picking on him. It's similar to inviting a child into dinner, but then every time he reaches over to eat, he gets smacked in the head with a spoon. It wouldn't be long after, that when you open the door to the dining room, he will be waiting on the other side of the door ready to retaliate for the abuse.

*If I were working with
Dream today, I'd handle him
completely differently.
What I do now surprises
a lot of people. I am
constantly learning from
past experiences and I
continue to change my
methods as I see something
more productive evolve.
I try to use more loving
techniques. Soon after,
the horse discovers that it's
a pleasant experience to
have a human enter his
stall, and the circle of
violence can be broken.*

Dream had gathered up the new mares with the original ones, and was keeping the young studs and geldings huddled away.

As John realized what had obviously taken place, he knew that Dream could not have merely slipped through the fence unscathed. The pastures were all barbed wire fences—pretty standard at the time—even though barbed wire had been designed for the tough hides of cattle, not the sensitive coat of the horse. When he walked up to Dream, he stopped short and caught his breath. Dream's chest was entirely ripped open across where both shoulders meet the chest muscle. The wire had cut through deep enough to where John could have put his hand into the sliced muscle. The skin was hanging loose over that cut and his chest was shredded to ribbons. John raced up to the house to call the veterinarian. He arrived thirty minutes later and sewed his skin and flesh back together. It took nearly 350 separate stitches to close up Dream's injuries.

That event spoke volumes for Dream's character and his mind-set. Dream basically had drawn a line in the sand, stating that if anyone were to fight with him, perhaps over mares, or perhaps just for dominance, that horse individual would have to be willing to suffer more than Dream had. Dream had been willing not only to shred his flesh to get into a pasture for new mares, but to ignore his intense pain to separate the other studs and geldings out.

It's not impossible to run across a horse who can fight better than most people can. The more a person whips, flogs, or spurs him, the tougher he will get. This horse quickly associates pain with all humans, and each encounter with a person becomes a battle. Often, aggressive horses are punished—out of human fear—for behavior they haven't even committed.

Punishment, rather than correction, happens to a lot of stallions, and John strove to find a way to break that pattern when he met up with Dream. The method John used didn't include a chain over his nose for control, although it did involve a whip. This was a long, soft buggy whip used not to beat a horse, but to tap against a horse's front legs as an annoyance rather than to elicit pain. When John led Dream around, Dream took large, assertive strides to get in front of John. John then tapped Dream below the knees, which made the horse take a step back and move behind. Dream lowered his head, which made it near impossible to rear, and soon learned to hang back. Because John used the whip as an extension of his arm, he was able to tap Dream without turning his whole body, allowing him to gain more control over the training session.

John got into the routine of tapping him three times—rap, rap, rap—and nothing more. If one tap got Dream's attention, John would cease. Sometimes it took two taps. Three was the maximum number of taps ever delivered to Dream. And there was a good reason.

Dream could do the math. He understood what John was trying to accomplish, and he could count how many times he got tapped for stepping into John's space. During one session, just as John thought that he had the horse fixed to lead properly, Dream once again forged ahead. In frustration, John tapped—one, two, three…four. Dream instantly knew. It was as if he understood that three was a correction, but four was abuse. He opened his mouth, teeth bared, and lunged at John, pushing him over and knocking him to the ground. He bit him squarely and galloped off. John also learned to count more carefully after that.

From 1977 to 1996, John worked with thousands of horses, and each one helped him modify his methods. His original way to cure biting was effective, but it was quickly replaced by ever increasing kinder, gentler methods that used more equine psychology. Over the years, he studied equine behavior, learned to read the horse's body language better, and experimented.

One of John's first methods to cure biting was also good both for horses who had a habit of rubbing against their handlers and those who nipped owners who weren't paying attention to them. John believed that these horses acted up because they wanted attention, being the extremely social creatures that they are, and so he gave it out in bundles. He would begin by rubbing the horse's face all over. First the horse would stand for the rubbing, but then it would begin to wear on him, and the horse would become restless. John continued to "kill him with kindness," stroking and rubbing the horse's face. In a very short time, the horse who was originally being bossy and rubbing against his handler would be irritated from all the attention and then keep a good distance.

The next of John's original cures for aggressive, biting horses was the three-second rule. When a horse bit his handler (or pulled other dangerous behavior such as kicking or striking), that person had three seconds to mete out the swiftest punishment possible, declaring war. It had to be put into the horse's mind that he had made the biggest mistake he ever could, and that he was going to pay for his actions. This cure was based on herd behavior. When two horses fight and one kicks at the other hard, that horse is telling the other in no uncertain terms that he's

In John's Words

Training continues to evolve. When I started doing the clinics, I used to tell people that if they rode in a clinic one year and then came back six months later and saw me doing exactly the same thing in another clinic, they shouldn't ever come back again. To me, that meant I'd been spinning my wheels for the last six months, not learning anything new, and no one wants to pay money for the same information. Every method, even today, that I use has room to improve and become better. I might not know it right now, but there's a better way to do everything, and I intend to keep searching for it.

Breeder Joe didn't have a clue how he solved the problem. But the first breeder followed the person who had developed the problem, not the one who solved it. We don't see how Joe solved the problem, and Joe doesn't even know. He just thinks his horse has a great disposition. The very best way to solve the biting problem is to hang all over their heads. Love on them while they're eating, stick your hands all over their faces, play with them—it's amazing how fast the horse comes around. This,

(Continued at right)

angry. John felt that this method wasn't as vicious as what horses dealt out to each other in real life, since it would be nearly impossible to hit with the velocity of a horse's kick. But there were rules. A person could not hit a horse in any way that would leave a mark on him or permanently hurt him because that would certainly be abuse. Additionally, a person could not hit a horse in the face, which could make the horse head shy for life, as sometimes happens. Finally, the punishment had to take place within three seconds of the behavior—any longer and the horse wouldn't remember what the punishment was for.

John liked to use the analogy of the three neighboring horse breeders. The first breeder has just acquired a stud who bites, and so he goes to his neighbor Joe to ask him how to solve the problem. The two walk over to Joe's stallion, who is an absolute pussycat, and Joe pats the horse's head, plants a big kiss on his nose, and lavishes him with attention, saying, "You know, I'm clueless. This stallion has always been like this, since he was a young colt. I just love on him and hug him, and I think it's just his disposition."

Well, Joe seems to be of no help to the owner of the biting stud, so he travels to Jake's ranch. Jake is ready to get his stallion out of his stall. He quickly gets a halter over the stud's head and a chain over his nose. The horse is led out by Jake jerking hard on the stud chain, and the stud is biting and striking out in retaliation. Jake yells to his neighbor, "Get back! This crazy horse has always been like this, we've had to do this since he was a baby." So the first breeder leaves, believing that the second method is how you handle a stud.

The first breeder goes home, puts the chain over his horse's nose, scolds him, yanks at him, and in a very short manner of time, he has a horse identical to Jake's. After all, he used the same training method that Jake did.

Once Dream had his issues worked out, John began to train him under saddle in earnest. He rode him daily and took him on the road, performing at clinics and symposiums all over the nation. As Dream became a better riding horse, John grew even closer to him. The training sessions were difficult, but John felt they both had come very far together. Dream was still a horse with his own mind, and he could probably never be dominated, but John believed it was a true relationship. He spent more time working with Dream than he did with any other horse because though Dream kept improving, John never felt he could completely relax around him.

And it wasn't all just work. John took that terrible habit of biting and turned it into a game that they both shared. Many people didn't know about Dream's history as a bad biter, and they believed that because he was John's horse, he was completely safe. This was very dangerous, since people at the shows would just go right on up to Dream and start petting him. So John decided to teach Dream to stick out his own tongue by shaking his fist at him. He would first shake his fist and then stick his thumb in Dream's mouth, making him stick out his tongue. When Dream closed down on his tongue, John fussed over him. That was all the positive reinforcement Dream needed. Any time John shook his fist at Dream, he would stick out his tongue in order to get the reward of John hugging and petting him.

Audiences loved it. Dream craved the attention and began to use his tongue as a cue to tell John when he wanted attention. John made afternoon visits to the barn, and the big bay would stick out his tongue for hugs and pats. "After a while, that horse had me trained to do what *he* wanted," John said.

One night, after a weeklong clinic, John visited the hosting barn. The stable was nearly empty. He walked down the dimly lit barn aisle to where Zip and Dream were housed. John watched in amazement as he saw the two stallions nose to nose with a bar partition separating them, each taking turns making faces and sticking out their tongues at each other. Zip had never been a mouthy horse and had never even gotten nippy for treats. But the two had turned the behavior into a game of tag, and that was the cue for horseplay. John had taught Dream a behavior that was not natural in order to get attention, and Dream, in turn, had taught a fellow horse.

In 1991, just two years after John had begun doing symposiums, Dream was about fourteen years old and had become a regular fixture with John and Zip in the symposium demonstrations. One Sunday night, John and his son, Josh, left Parachute, Colorado, and drove up through Utah, and into Idaho. They had worked all day at a symposium in Utah, and had driven into early the next morning, but John had another show in Oregon to get to. John had just bought a big moving van that would help him carry all of his equipment and two horses. He had been working on redesigning it, packing all of the equipment in the back, and building a partition to keep the two horses separate from the equipment.

The roads in Idaho were often just two-lane highways. On this part of the journey, bright orange cones denoted that the highway

I believe, stems from the knowledge that horses are very social creatures. They love to love and be loved. They are not cows that could care less about seeing a human. They are animals who live to serve man and they want to please us. They are, in my opinion, God's favorite animals because he mentions them more than any other animal in the Bible, except for sheep. God also talks about how He will be riding a white horse when He returns. Horses are meant to be loved by us.

That was a terribly hard time. I learned some awfully important things from my whole relationship with that horse. It's amazing what I would do over with Dream if I could. It's funny, because the last memory I have of riding Dream, I was up in the mountains. The top of the ridge is my very favorite place to ride. It's beautiful— the grass is belly deep in these hundred-acre meadows, and there are huge pine forests to ride through. So there I was, riding in some of the most picturesque countryside, but instead of enjoying the view and the aroma of the pines, I'm focused on training. I worked Dream hard, on some very complex material that required him to concentrate fully, and it was no different than if I were in an arena.

(Continued at right)

was under construction, and John noticed there was no shoulder on the side of the road and just a drop-off to a slope.

It was early morning and John was exhausted. He fought to keep his eyes open as he drove the huge truck, but it was impossible. He dozed off at the wheel—only for a second—and the truck drifted over one lane, and then slipped off the road. With no shoulder at the road's edge, the truck plunged down the drop-off for about 15 feet and flipped over on its side. John and Josh were a little dazed and bruised, but unhurt. Thinking of the horses, John rushed to the back of the truck and pried open the door. Zip was miraculously uninjured. Dream, however, was not so lucky. He was lying trapped, with a huge gaping wound that started from the top of his right haunch all the way down to his hock. The flesh hung open and he was bleeding profusely.

In the morning light, John wedged open the back doors and began to furiously throw out the round pen, speakers, tack, and gear onto the highway. Then he tore out the wall to free the horses, who had to be able to stand up before they could get out.

A gentleman driving a cattle trailer saw the wreckage by the side of the road and stopped to help. He offered to take the injured horse into the next town so he could see a vet. After John had freed both horses from the back of the moving van, he carefully loaded the ailing Dream into the trailer with Zip, and rode in the back with him for the 100-mile trip to the vet. They left all the equipment and the torn-up truck on the side of the road, worrying only about getting Dream some care.

The vet on call worked on Dream for many hours. John stayed with him all day and that night, and then, thoroughly spent, finally got to a motel room the following night. Meanwhile, one of John's road staff drove up from Colorado and got a tow truck to pick up the wrecked truck and equipment.

After that horrific accident, everyone wanted John to quit and return home. They still had 700 miles to go to Oregon, and only two days left to travel, arrive, set up, and get ready for the symposium. All the equipment was still 100 miles back down the road, and although John's truck was not totaled, it needed some hefty repairs and would never be ready in time.

But John didn't want to quit. He needed to fulfill that Oregon date, and it wouldn't do any good to watch Dream in recovery every day. He decided to rent a U-Haul as a last resort. He carefully loaded the equipment in the front portion of the U-Haul truck, then took a round pen panel and put it across the back, to divide the truck in half. John got Zip to jump up into the back of the truck and away they went, with Zip looking out the back of a U-Haul.

John got to Oregon and set up with just moments to spare. After the show, he drove from southern Oregon to Seattle, Washington, for the next weekend's symposium. He still needed his truck, which was ready to be picked up back in Idaho. A couple of volunteers drove all the way from Washington back to Idaho to pick up the repaired truck and bring it back up to Washington so John could carry on with the symposium.

Dream's recovery was going well back in Idaho. He handled his convalescence with a good attitude, despite the fact that he had to stand cross-tied in a thickly bedded stall for more than two weeks. When the vets commented on what a sweet horse Dream was the whole time, John had a pretty good idea how much pain Dream must have been in. Over the years, Dream had developed navicular disease, but his recuperation made the pain in his hooves more acute. After standing on his hurting feet for fourteen days, the vet finally untied him in his stall and allowed him to lie down in the soft bedding.

Dream luxuriated in the ability to finally get off his feet and be comfortable, and he took a long nap stretched out on his side. But when he awoke, he struggled to rise, and in his awkward thrashing to protect his still-healing hip and hock, he lurched forward clumsily. It was a grave mistake. The other leg was unable to support his large body properly, and the pressure made a small bone break in his left leg.

The vet heard the commotion and sedated Dream. He applied a cast to the injured leg. Dream continued his recovery in the hospital, but it was a tremendous setback. Horses have a hard time recovering from leg injuries because of always needing to be on their feet, and with two injured legs, Dream was having a tough time of it. Dream had always been a massive horse, built like a tank in comparison to Zip. His build was making it all the more difficult to recover.

Two weeks later, the worst was realized. Dream tried to rise once again after a nap, and in his attempt to protect the leg with a cast on it, he shattered a bone in the opposite leg. There was no choice but to put Dream down. John was devastated but gave the vet permission to put the grand horse to sleep. He knew it was the only answer, but it still didn't make it any easier to lose him. Because he had worked so hard with Dream, and that horse had become one of his greatest teachers, John's heart was broken.

It was over a year before someone could even mention the horse's name without John's eyes filling up with tears and his chest tightening.

If I'd known it was going to be our last ride together, I would have done it differently. We would have just spent time together, enjoying the country, taking in the smell of the trees and watching this glorious sunset. I learned that we have to be careful with the time that we have. We can't let those thoughts of work or goals completely rule our lives. We shouldn't be afraid to step out from underneath them in order to do something different. We still have to have our working sessions and do what our everyday life calls for. But we need to recognize that we don't know when it's going to be over, that we don't have any guarantees, and it's important that while we work, we take moments to make sure that we enjoy what we are doing.

Chapter

7

THE SYMPOSIUM

The John Lyons Symposium attendees came from all walks of life. In the horse world where people are so diverse (and opinionated), the equestrian populous was eager to join together and embrace new training methods. Trail riders who'd logged many a mile in the saddle signed up. Newbies who had just bought their first horses also made up a big part of John's audience. The majority rode western, but he had his share of English riders, too. A small segment of the attendees were serious competitive riders, and John was amazed when trainers at the top levels and even Olympic-level riders were on the attendance roster. But what he liked best was seeing attendees who hadn't bought their first horse but wanted to get educated first.

John saw his audience change from when the symposiums were in their infancy. Where once he would look into the audience and see mostly novices, with a few ropers and cowboy stragglers, he later saw a pretty good sampling of the overall horse industry, all sitting in rapt attention, craving the knowledge.

The symposiums caught on quickly because the audience could easily see John, they were always protected from the weather, and John had more time to explain his training methods.

John tried different formats to determine the most effective way to reach people. He used everything from unbroken horses to his own well-trained horses to show the audience every kind of challenge. He learned there was no perfect format for the symposium, but that he had to address many different areas of training to satisfy the diverse needs of the attendees. After hundreds of symposiums, John knew people always yearned for more knowledge, as did he. He was spending more than forty-five weeks out of the year on the road, while Susie remained at the office, handling accounting, marketing, and public relations.

It wasn't just the audience who was catching on. Fellow trainers from around the nation were also watching—with great interest. They saw what John was doing, and began to follow suit with their own brand of clinics. Some taught winning equitation that would garner championships. Some promised to "ride an unbroken horse in thirty minutes or less." Others maybe saw a chance to raise their profile, maybe even get a little peek at stardom. Some were solid horsemen, but there were one or two who had no business teaching horse or rider. The possibility of money or fame—or perhaps a bit of both—kept the trainers busy.

But John went about his own business while all this was taking place and worked on his large symposiums the same way he had handled his smaller clinics. While he diligently honed his training methods, he never rehearsed to go in front of an audience. In fact, most sessions were impromptu—tailored to the group that filled the seats. It was true he promoted a range of topics to be covered, such as fixing spooky horses, high-headed horses, or resistant mounts, but he never had a routine down pat. He'd just walk into the ring and begin speaking, and the information would pour out—informally, engagingly. And whatever questions came from the audience would be responded to on the fly. The queries from the audience usually caused him to go past break times, lunch times, and late into the evening hours. It seemed as though there was never enough time to get all the information out.

In 1987, John was contacted by the Farnam Company, one of the largest horse-care companies in the world, to put out a video. Farnam chose the main subject of the video—working with an unbroken horse—and John added training solutions for head shyness. Over the course of four days in Litchfield, Arizona, he completed one of the industry's first training videos, *Round Pen Reasoning*. A second video

about trailer loading and teaching leading programs followed a year later. Both videos became classics and a popular way for people to learn from John.

Performing at multiple symposiums became the norm in John's life. Dozens of people approached him after every session to tell him how he'd made a difference to their horse.

"Your symposium was the best training seminar I've ever attended. . . . You taught me more in two days than I've learned in a lifetime."

"John, you're a fantastic teacher. . . . You break every technique down into simple steps so I can understand exactly what you're doing. My horse is so much more responsive now to everything I ask."

"I never expected that when I went home from the symposium I could actually get my horse to be calmer and willingly do whatever I asked....The exercises are so simple yet they work."

"My horse has overcome so many fears by using the techniques I learned at the symposium. . . . She's calmer on the trail and now when she gets excited I know exactly what to do."

"While I have never written the host of the many clinics I have attended in the past, I got so much from my two days spent with you I felt I should let you know. Not only was your information well put together and presented, but the genuine interest you showed in everyone there made me feel very comfortable. Because you put the extra effort in, encouraging the audience to take active part in your training, I was able to get up the courage to ask a few questions. . . . "

"You are still the talk of the town. . . . Next year I'll bring everyone I can round up."

As John honed his presentation and speaking skills, he kept these people in mind. Working on the road, he was a man focused. He used every opportunity to sharpen his techniques. Horses were not only his pupils but also his teachers. He talked to other trainers while traveling to gain insight into their programs.

One told him, "You know, I learn from every horse."

"You do?" John replied. "I'm not that smart. It seems like it took me sixty horses before I really got the lesson."

The trainer replied, "What are you talking about?"

John said, "Maybe it's that I was training these horses all the same way, but after interacting with dozens of horses, I would suddenly see something in a different light. Maybe a muscle moved differently, or one thing related to something else, and all of a sudden that opened up

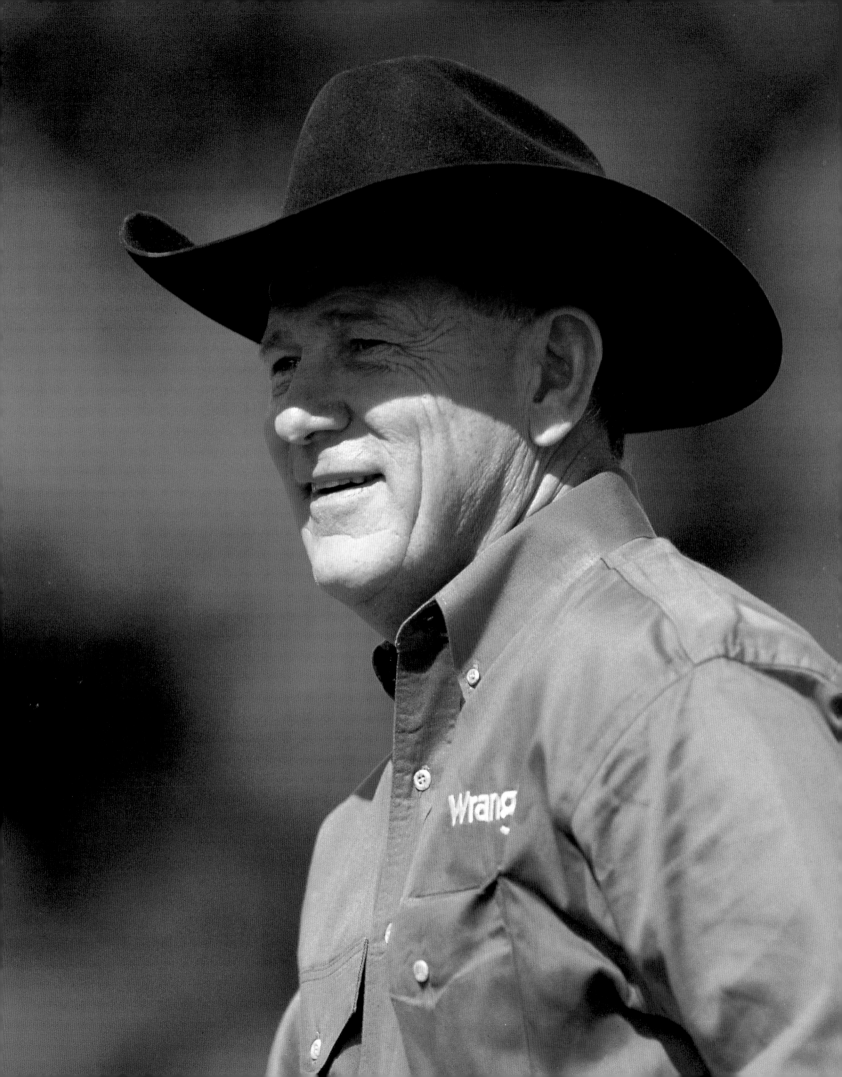

*The Cowboy
Up Ranch*

another doorway. And then I learned ten new things from that. It's funny but that's how the horses teach me!"

The curriculum changed as John grew as a teacher. He wanted his program to be better and more clearly understood. After one session, a rider came up to him with sort of a complaining tone. "John, this is weird. The last time you were teaching me a totally different way."

John replied, "I was teaching you what I knew yesterday, now I'm teaching you what I know today."

It kept training horses and doing symposiums exciting for him, and educational for the people who attended his symposiums year after year. He knew that if he had to teach the same thing the same way over and over, he would get burned out. And once burnout set in, all that was left was the paycheck at the end of the day. He remembered the days in Kansas City when he had the fat annual salary but no fulfillment. For him, that life was never enough—he needed more to be satisfied. This was especially true with the tough schedule he was adhering to.

Toward the end of each year, Susie and John would have their biggest fights because that was the time John would begin to schedule his next year of being on the road. They would sit down in the office and begin to outline their year. "We gotta make these numbers come out right," John would tell Susie.

"You're booking too many dates. I'll never see you," she would say.

"But financially this is the only way to do it. Sure, there are a lot of pieces to the puzzle. I just have to get all of them to fit together," John would argue. They would work late into the night until exhausted. But one of the reasons why John started the symposiums in the first place was so he eventually wouldn't have to be on the road as much. But since the first symposiums didn't exactly go according to plan—with John $90,000 in the hole after the first year—he had to schedule more than 35 symposiums for the second year. He kept telling Susie that eventually they'd have time left over.

So they had to live a year in advance. When most people didn't plan anything other than where they'd spend their two-week vacations, John knew exactly where he would be on March 25 of the following year. It was tough to be utterly locked into an unyielding schedule. Even more difficult was the fact that once the commitment was made, John and his crew had to show up—there was no flexibility in the schedule to postpone dates—nor was there any tolerance for sick days. The show had to go on. And to this day, John has never missed one single show.

John added two-week clinics at his Cowboy Up Ranch. He also tried to vary the schedule, with sixteen three- and four-day clinics nationwide scheduled right after the symposium, so he could offer a format for people wanting to work their horses with John.

For the next couple of years, John's schedule averaged thirty-five to forty-two individual dates, an exhausting schedule by any stretch of the imagination. His routine was to set up on Friday morning for an evening question and answer program, then work all day Saturday and Sunday. He would then have his clinics from Monday through Wednesday, and spend all day Thursday driving, usually 500 miles on average. The process would begin again with the setup the next Friday. It took five years to get out of the debt they incurred their first year of doing symposiums. But at what price?

Chapter

8

TOUCHING HORSES,
TOUCHING LIVES

There are as many behavioral and training problems

for horses as there are fixes. And John knew that people struggled to find the one solution that would be the answer to their particular difficulties.

In order to get people to attend his clinics, John offered a money back guarantee if the riders were not satisfied with their horses' results. If John could not completely satisfy the attendee, he did not get paid. This proved to be a major stepping stone in John's training because he learned that every problem with a horse can be fixed. The guarantee kept John thinking on his feet and always looking for easier, better solutions. In addition to the money back guarantee, John also followed two other guidelines for his clinics. He only had a limited amount of time to work with the horse during the clinic, and he had to use methods that were approved by the owner of the horse. Through these rules, he learned to work every horse to the satisfaction of the owner using the kindest methods possible.

Sometimes John would have fifteen horses to work with during a three day clinic. He felt an enormous amount of pressure at first, trying to "save them all," but decided that he needed to focus on one horse at a time—to concentrate solely on working with that horse first.

He told clinic attendants, "It's important for me that the first horse I work with, I get fixed. Now I know that means there's a chance that I might not get to your horse by the time the clinic is over. If that happens, you'll get your money back. But I have to make sure that I solve this one's problems before I go on to the next."

Attendees would nod in agreement: it was the best solution. With the pressure off, and by reassuring owners and riders that they wouldn't ever be slighted, John was free to concentrate on the task at hand. He methodically trained each horse as an individual and was able to finish his work with every horse. Not one person asked for his or her money back.

Still, "satisfaction guaranteed" in a business as unpredictable as horse training was a challenge. There were plenty of times when John had to think on his feet. The Eau Claire, Michigan, clinic—unlike his clinics in the Southwest—was attended by a variety of riders, including two local upper-level dressage trainers who brought a couple of large warmblood geldings with them. The size of these European horses was tremendous—both easily stood at 17 hands at the withers. The first trainer began to describe his gelding's training challenge. "There's no *schwung* in this horse's stride. He's tight over his topline, and I can't get him light on the bit without losing throughness."

John stared blankly at the trainer, and then the rider. *What in the heck is he talking about?* John wondered. "Well, maybe I should just get on and see for myself," John finally said.

The trainer nodded and saddled up the horse. John swung into the deep dressage saddle, with its high pommel and cantle and its long stirrups. After adjusting them up to his leg, he gathered up the reins and cued the horse forward. The horse immediately hollowed his back and pushed his nose skyward as he walked. John thought, *Ah ha! This is easy to fix.*

Within a short period, John had the horse moving forward off his leg with energy and a swing to his stride. The warmblood was carrying himself, propelling forward from his hindquarters, over his back, and into the bridle, staying light and responsive to John's hand. Bingo! There was the *schwung*—the swinging, energetic stride—and the throughness the trainer was seeking. One down, one to go.

The next trainer began to describe her horse's training problem, again using the dressage terminology that was so confusing to John. John interrupted her. "Lady, I'm just off the ranch. I have no clue what you're talking about. Just tell me in English what you want the feet to do. I can then get the horse to do what you want."

She burst out in peels of laughter. "I'm sorry, John! I suppose I was sounding like a dressage queen, now wasn't I?" That horse did his canter pirouette perfectly by the end of the day.

John actually used the Bible as a basis for some of the principles in his training, just like in his life. It helped him to understand and appreciate what he could and couldn't do. It taught John that the people were more important than the horse in the problem-solving equation.

"It's not just solving the horse's problem," he'd tell Susie, "I can do that all day long. What I really have to get better at is listening to the people and understanding what their troubles are, and then I will have what I need to fix the horse."

John used the book of James often when looking for inspiration. Although it is one of the shorter books of the Bible, John was able to extract more than a dozen analogies that could be applied to horse training and giving his clinics. John really took James 3:2-3. Authorized King James Version (AV) to heart. "For in many things we offend all. If any man offend not in word, the same is a perfect man, and able also to bridle his whole body. Behold, we put bits in the horses' mouths, that they may obey us; and we turn about their whole body."

The passage was special to John because it noted that people should not be like the stubborn horse who needs to be controlled by a bridle and bit. Instead, they should be responsive to different cues that God gives them. John experimented with the meaning by literally teaching Zip to ride bridleless.

Zip was so light and responsive to cues that John successfully got him to do all of the same things he did with a bridle. It became a highlight at his symposiums to show the different things he could get Zip to do just by using leg cues and his seat.

Moderation was key, however, and John found that doing so many different demonstrations bridleless had its pitfalls. John found that a horse ridden a great deal without a bridle begins to pin his ears, swish his tail, and travel rather uncollected. John discovered that his legs and feet are actually annoying to the horse, and it took Zip quite a bit of effort to understand what John wanted. When John finally realized this, that verse began to take on a whole new meaning. James 3:3 actually revealed to him that, ultimately, a rider should use the bridle and bit in conjunction with the seat and leg and not just one without the other.

John also used Scripture for parallels in both life and training. In the Bible it states that where there is no movement, there is no life. John knew it was talking about his Christian walk. People could have an outward appearance of being a Christian, but if there was no movement toward God, they were not really living for Christ. And with horses, the one ingredient that he had to have to train a horse was, of course, movement. "I can't even teach a horse to stand still or stop without movement," John would say at his clinics. "You have to be able to get him to go in order to teach him to stop."

John took to heart James 2:2-8 because it said not to treat one person better than the other, using the parable of giving the wealthy man the best seat in church, while the beggar was relegated to the back. It was not only important to be fair to all his clients, but by treating everyone alike, equal treatment also helped keep him safe. John was occasionally pressured to spend more time on certain clients because they brought their more expensive horse to the clinic or because they were important show competitors. Even though John made it a point to treat each horse and rider team with the same respect that each deserved, sometimes it didn't suit a few clients.

At a clinic in Georgia, a local rider brought her young futurity prospect for John to work with because the stud was a biter. This horse was a classy bay with two white socks. The owner said, "I spent a lot of money on this horse. He cost me $20,000 as a two-year-old, and I've invested another couple grand in training him. You be careful with him—I don't want to see this horse hurt." John nodded, and took the lead rope.

John found that in trying to be too careful with the horse, he was actually putting himself at risk. As she kept interjecting, "No, don't do that, you might hurt him," John explained to her, "You're not the one climbing in the round pen, taking this risk. No matter how expensive this horse is, I'm going to treat him exactly the same as I would that person's horse over there, who was rescued at an auction," he said. He made his point—the horse shouldn't be treated differently just because he had a high price tag, and John was not going to risk getting hurt just because an owner wanted her horse handled with kid gloves. The colt had a problem—a common problem—and John saw fit to correct that problem in a safe and effective manner. She understood finally, and sat back to watch John work with her horse.

James 1:8 says that a double-minded man is unstable in all ways, like a boat being tossed to and fro without a rudder on the ocean. John took that to the core of his training. He interpreted this to mean that he needed to be precise and clear in his signals to the horse. He couldn't be wishy-washy, and had to remain specific with what he said.

You'll read a verse in the Bible, and it says "do one thing." And it means something completely different to you than it does to me. Someone else reads it at a different time in his or her life, and it means something completely different to him or her, but it's the same ten words. So that's what it's like. I may have not changed a bit in what I am doing when I train a horse, but all of a sudden I will see it differently. And because I see it differently, it opens up a door to a whole new area of the horse's performance.

Because of his faith, John was guided through the tough times. But more than that, the Bible helped him deal with the people, the pressure of being on the road, and the crazy lifestyle that he was now embracing.

One of the biggest pressures was dealing with an audience. Whatever occurred—good or bad—happened in front of a crowd. John always made sure that his lessons and clinics were safe, but occasionally there would be a disaster. Most were a result of something completely unexpected.

One of the worst wrecks that John was ever involved in happened in front of more than three hundred participants and spectators in Pomona, California. One of the participants had brought in a beautiful, unbroke two-year-old Appaloosa colt. He was a halter horse with gorgeous conformation and a lovely disposition. John had worked him in the round pen once already, and everything had gone beautifully. The colt was a quick study and very curious. John did a lot of work from the back of Zip in the round pen. He'd used this method a thousand times before and had even included a great deal of this methodology in his *Round Pen Reasoning* video.

First, John worked the colt from the ground, getting him used to things around his body and eventually got the saddle on him. John then walked out to get Zip and bring him in the round pen. As soon as Zip entered, the young stud came over and tried to mount him. John chased him off and went to get his rope for the next lesson. He looked back as the colt began chasing Zip around the pen at a leisurely lope and then proceeded to bury his nose in Zip's rump.

Zip kicked out in surprise—not a powerful kick, just a reflex. There was a terrible popping noise. The kick had hit the young horse in the front leg in just the wrong spot, and the dreadful sound was the bone snapping. Stopping abruptly, the colt wore a quizzical expression as he stood, leg dangling below the knee. The spectators collectively gasped, and a few women yelped in horror. One of John's crew ran to the barn office to call a vet. Zip stopped loping as soon as he didn't feel the presence of the colt, and then turned and faced him. John stood in shock for a few moments, hardly believing his eyes. Then he walked as quickly as he could to the colt so that he could keep him quiet and still.

The stud colt was perfectly fine, and stood patiently with John at his halter. He was bright-eyed and quiet, not seemingly in any pain. The audience was still gathered around the round pen, a sea of faces looking helpless and stunned. John could hear the murmurs plainly.

"It wasn't a mean kick."

"That was a freak accident."

"Poor colt."

"Oh, my God...how terrible!"

The vet was nearby and arrived within twenty minutes, but John already knew what the outcome would be. There would be no setting of that compound fracture. By that time John and his staff had asked the audience to take a break and leave the arena for some privacy. John stood with the owner and the horse as the vet told them what they already knew.

The vet then gave the horse his first injection of pentobarbital, which suppressed the horse's central nervous system. This made the colt fall to the ground with a heavy thud, and he lost consciousness. The second shot of a barbiturate was administered, and a single heartbeat sent the drug swiftly to the colt's brain to depress all of its functions. The parts of the brain that controlled his breathing and heartbeat ceased to function in less than a minute, and all that was left of the colt was his lifeless form.

John felt helpless with the owner standing at his side. He quietly said, "I—I'm so sorry! This is so horrible. I can't tell you how badly I feel," he began.

Eyes brimming with tears, the owner choked out, "Zip barely touched him. I know that. It's nobody's fault." She sobbed, and John consoled her. The entire crowd was upset, but surprisingly, they were also supportive.

John knew he would be fighting a losing battle trying to justify any part of it. He told the owner, "You know, I have to accept responsibility completely. It wasn't the colt's fault, and it wasn't Zip's fault." He knew that if he had tried to pass the buck people would have started to take sides. Some critics might have said that his method was already an accident waiting to happen, and that John had no business putting two studs in a pen together. But Zip had been used in that exercise with dozens of other horses, from studs to geldings to mares, and the horse's gender had nothing to do with it. It wasn't like the two horses were galloping along madly either—it was just a slow western pleasure–style lope of two horses playing. It wasn't even a powerful kick, and neither horse had ears flattened or teeth bared. It was a terrible event, but it was a freak accident, and one that would probably never happen again. And because John accepted responsibility with an honest reaction and didn't try to justify it, the audience understood.

In John's Words

That was probably the worst situation that I've ever had to deal with. Learning how to handle those things and being quick to accept the situation in front of an audience is very difficult. However, that day I learned that as long as I answer honestly and from the heart, the audience will understand. I did my best to learn how not to react to those who are looking for me to come back at them and argue. Those clinicians of the late seventies and early eighties— the horsemen of the original clinics—had to learn how to deal with crazy, horrific situations like that, and they paved the way for a lot of today's clinicians and speakers. Most guys today don't have the opportunity to learn how to deal with a crisis, before they hold a demonstration or clinic in front of an audience.

It's like you're in this pitch black room and you find yourself groping along an expansive wall for what seems an eternity. Suddenly you find the door and reach for where the doorknob is. When you feel that there is a keyhole, you peer down to look through it and you can see something on the other side. That gives you insight, to know that there is something there that makes you see things in a different way.

You jiggle the doorknob and finally get the door to swing open. When you walk through, you find yourself in a room with endless opportunities, dozens of activities. It is like horse training. Here you are, groping with the same stuff, but then when you get one tiny insight, you suddenly see everything in a different way. You see the movement differently, the reaction differently. That one element unlocks the door to understanding.

Putting the incident out of his mind was difficult. He was haunted by the events but also knew that he had to keep moving forward. He threw himself back into his work, even more determined to make his interactions with horses and people the best they could be. His schedule never let up. That tragedy eventually was replaced with new, inspiring sessions. There were times that were little breakthrough moments while he was on the road.

With so many horses passing through his life, though, he became immersed in each training episode to the point where he didn't stop to analyze why that method was successful. But what was happening was that the more time he spent with horses, the more his understanding became innate, and his success came more naturally, more quickly. He was working with a paint horse who didn't like his ears being handled at all. The paint would raise his head high and fight when anyone came near him. He was impossible to clip, and every time his owner tried to bridle him, the fight would get longer. So John began his session with the horse. Instead of immediately starting to handle the horse's head or tying him up so that he couldn't escape John's efforts, he began to run his hands all over the horse's body—his hips, legs, and feet. He used an exercise he liked to call the WESN lesson, which teaches the horse to move in all four directions (West, East, South, and North) with the lead rope, because the horse obviously had problems with being led and giving to pressure. During this session, he never touched the horse's face or ears. He simply spent an hour working on little exercises on the ground that would help get the horse responsive to leading better. At the end of the hour and a half session, he smoothly moved to the horse's head and began to stroke and pat it, then caressed the ears. He was able to gently place his fingers inside the furry ear canals and touch the pointy tops, all within a couple of minutes. He ran his hand through the forelock, and the horse even lowered his head in response. The owner was absolutely thrilled.

John went home that night and had an epiphany. Even when an owner told him what the horse's specific problem was—unwillingness to pick up feet, touchy around the ears, spooky about fly spray—John never went directly to the problem. Instead, he started somewhere else with the horse, in an area completely unrelated. By the time that he actually made a move to address the specific problem, John had already founded a relationship with the horse, had established control, and in return, the horse had given John respect and trust. John also did his best to make sure all training sessions were pain-free, trouble-free, and without trauma. By the time he addressed the problem that the owner requested him to address, the horse was already more comfortable and could be handled easily.

Chapter

9

A FIRM FAITH

When John was a little boy, he always had a feeling
that God had something meaningful for him to do with his life. He knew
God was close by and that his life had a purpose, yet he never could quite
figure out what he was meant to do. Some fellow Christians went into the
ministry, while others took the road to become missionaries. John,
however, was not sure what was in store for him.

He felt in his heart that his goal wasn't to be important, famous, or
special. Instead, he had a feeling that perhaps he'd be at the right place
at the right time, maybe to save someone from the path of a speeding car
so that person could go on to do something great for God. During those
younger years, he believed that he would grow up and be a catalyst for
someone else—to say something at the right time, which would set off a
chain of events for another person to do something really important.

It wasn't until 1996 that he discovered his calling. Since his symposiums ended on Sundays, John would schedule ministers or speakers
to do the morning church service; people such as Ted Presley from
Cowboys for Christ or Crystal and Ray Lyons, not related to John, but
both strong Christians involved in professional rodeo. He'd also get
people from the local ministries, such as Randy and Russ Weaver, to give
their testimonies to inspire people in the horse industry. Every once in a

That was the most amazing thing, to see everything that had happened over the past decades and look back at the steps that went into it. To see how He pulled it all together and that I would be chosen to help get this message across. In my opinion, there are many better trainers in the world. There are lots of better horsemen around, so it just doesn't make any sense that I've ended up with the popularity that I have. I found the reason that day in Arizona, watching the crowd at Sunday service.

while, John would step in and do the service when someone had to cancel or didn't show up. Something started to click inside him.

It was early fall in 1996 and John was in Scottsdale, Arizona, giving a weekend symposium like so many hundreds he'd done before. It was being held in an expansive covered arena, and there was a glorious desert sunrise just creeping up over the Saddleback Mountains. John had scheduled Crystal Lyons for the Sunday service. As Crystal began, John sat in the audience just listening intently, absorbing the beauty of the day. At that moment, he realized that his calling in life is to provide a vehicle for people who may not otherwise have the opportunity to go to church to hear God's word in a type of "cowboy" church service. It wasn't for him to preach or to witness; it was to provide the whole symposium, a horse training emporium that also included a time devoted to Christ and a place for people to hear His word. During that epiphany, John traced back several events during his life, and strangely enough he could see how at key points, God was always directing them.

It didn't make any sense, thought John, *that a person who wasn't raised in the saddle, didn't have a pony growing up, and didn't even own a horse until he was twenty-four, came to live on a ranch in Colorado and came up with the idea to work with horses.* It was so odd that he had ended up living on a cattle-less ranch, then somehow came up with the idea to work with horses. Even stranger was his natural—make that supernatural—affinity to work with these creatures. From training to giving clinics to starting up his innovative symposiums to becoming a megastar in the horse industry—John suddenly realized all the curious paths his life had to take to get to where he was that day.

Raised in a Southern Baptist home, John was given concrete Christian values and he accepted Christ into his life at an early age. Since the age of seven, John has known how close and real God is and how much God cares about people. Through the years, John felt close to God and felt Him guide his daily life. John also realized there are times when people grow apart from God, even though God never truly lets go of His people. Like close friends that may have just been reunited, John always felt his relationship with God grow stronger and deeper. John always knew he was never perfect, but always forgiven and wanted in God's eyes.

His faith has pervaded all aspects of his life, including work. John has used the Bible to help guide him during dark times, to inspire him to work diligently, to direct him with his family, and to aid him in dealing with people. It particularly affected the way he worked with horses.

John enjoyed telling the story, referring to Matt. 21:8-9., (AV), of when Jesus told His disciples to go to the edge of town and find a donkey mare, and beside her they would discover a colt whereon no man had ever sat. He told His disciples to take the colt, and if anyone questioned why they were taking him, to tell the owner that the Master needed him.

The owner of the colt saw the disciples taking him out of the pasture and asked what they were doing stealing his property. They replied that the Master needed the colt, and the owner said, "Take the colt then." The disciples brought the colt to Jesus. That very day the Lord was riding astride the unbroken colt in a parade of sorts.

John would explain that Jesus didn't have to do any training of the colt—through His power, the colt allowed Him to ride. Said John, "He was the only real horse whisperer who ever came down the pike."

Further explaining how equines are the Lord's favorite animal, John used the example of Balaam's donkey from Num. 22:20-33., (AV). The Lord blessed this donkey with a human voice on one occasion—the time when the donkey's master was flogging him. Balaam's donkey asked his master why he was beating him when he was only trying to help him.

And on what would God make His return to earth? The Scripture tells of the Lord riding a white horse in the book of Revelations. John would note that in Chapter Six there are multitudes of horses carrying His army, so in his mind this shows that there are horses in heaven.

John noted that God places many qualities that are important to Him in the horse. Like the artist who depicts beautiful subjects that stir his soul, inspire, and evoke, God, too, crafted the horse with qualities that He respected. John would explain how God is very much a God of order, and that one cannot look at the universe, see how everything fits together, and call it mere random acts. When He made the horse, He created a social animal because God likes togetherness. He made the horse a herd animal, but it's a very orderly process that horses live under. This is most easily seen in a herd situation during feeding time, where the pecking order is clearly evident when horses have their meal.

One of the most important characteristics a horse has is forgiveness. John would use the powerful example of a horse who has been mistreated daily for years until he is quite fearful of humans. A horse who is beaten regularly about the head will be utterly terrified when interacting with people. Yet a trainer who understands how horses think can come along and do two things to the horse so that he is no longer frightened of being approached around the head. The first, of course, is to stop the chain of

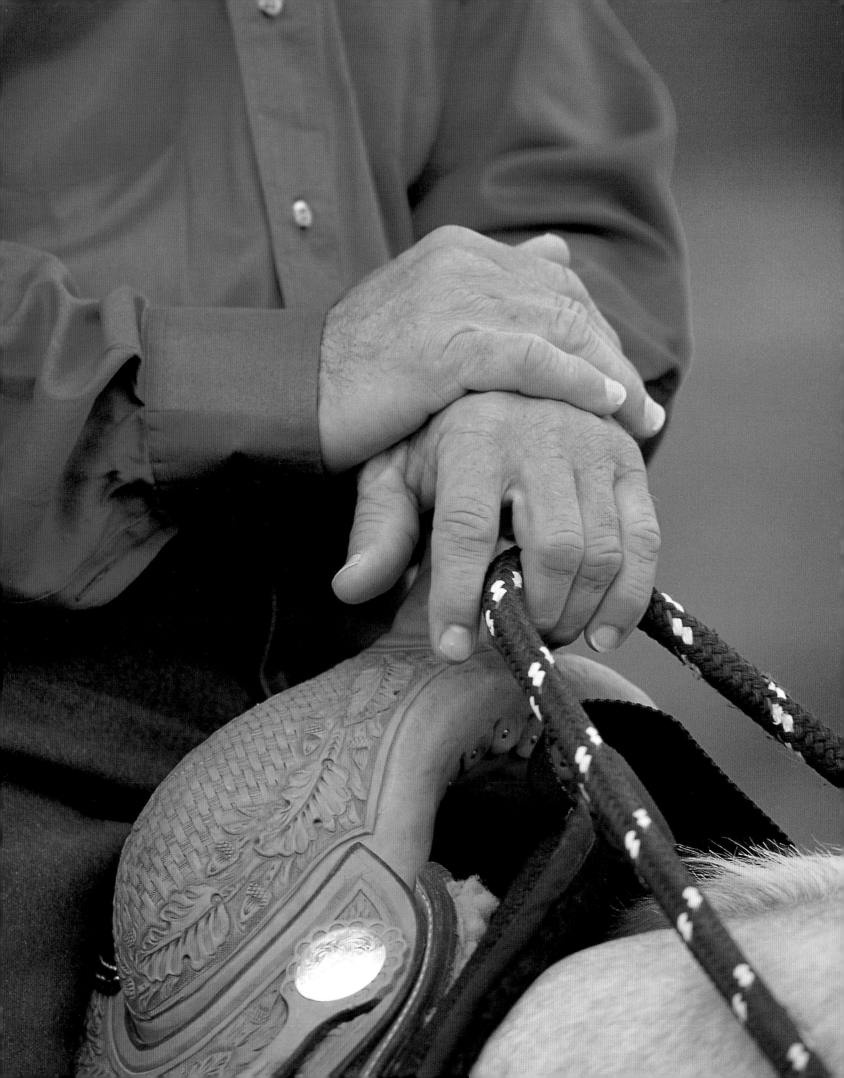

God likes people who can adapt and get along, and He made the horse with those very qualities. A horse can live in a tie-stall that is 36 inches wide and 8 feet long—like the kind they have in Europe—and as long as his need for food, exercise, and care are met, he can exist in that way his entire life and be quite content. Or he can pull a buggy down the streets of New York City, or he can jump 6-foot fences, or he can do ballet or spin or chase cattle. He can also do none of the above and live on a million acres in the middle of nowhere and take care of

(Continued at right)

abuse. Then the trainer needs to convince the horse to trust him and believe that he would never be hit in the head again. When the horse then allows his head to be touched, haltered, bridled, and his ears to be clipped, it doesn't necessarily mean that the horse has forgotten those years of abuse in a few short hours. Instead, John would say that the horse evaluates us and decides *I see you have changed, and because you have changed I will not hold the past against you.* In John's eyes, that mirrors God's forgiveness.

While God's love is unconditional, His forgiveness is very conditional. The condition is that people will admit that they are wrong, that they will try to change, and that they accept Jesus Christ into their lives. The moment that a person does this, God will forgive us. Using this parallel, John would say that there is no such thing as a ruined horse. When people brought a horse to him who was a complete rogue, John would persevere until that horse was fixed. A horse trainer can always go in and work with a damaged horse, and that animal can change his behavior and adapt and become whole again.

John would say that the Lord gave the horse a tremendous amount of courage and the ability to overcome fear. Most people have the perception that a horse is a timid, fearful animal. The horse is a prey animal and does have a very well preserved flight instinct, but people don't realize that some of the tasks that they ask of their horses are actually life and death decisions. John uses the example of getting a horse to cross a creek as a tremendous act of courage. People discount the horse's fear because they know the creek is shallow and easy to ford. To the horse, however, it's not the dislike of getting wet, it's the fear of stepping in and drowning. Of course, many people will give the horse no time at all to evaluate the water, to stick a foot in and test the bottom, to be assured that the icy stream will not carry him away. Impatient people will push their horses and whip and spur to get them through. Yet with the proper introduction to water, the horse can overcome his fear and trust his rider to know what is best for the two. He will bravely cross the stream—in spite of his instincts, which are telling him not to.

And John knows firsthand about the courage a horse must have to face the unknown. In 1995, Zip was given a routine injection of an antibacterial medication called Naxcel that was given to treat a cold. The drug had been used countless times on thousands of horses—and even Zip had been treated with it in the past. But this time, Zip had a reaction to the drug. When John administered the last injection in a series of five, Zip's body had a violent reaction. He went into a seizure and then fell to the ground, drifting in and out of consciousness for nearly thirty minutes. John's beloved partner, his horse with whom he had shared so many miles on the road, so many successes and setbacks, was in grave trouble.

Zip came to shortly after and finally struggled to his feet. John let him stand for a moment, then gently escorted him back into his stall and kept a close eye on him for the next few hours. Things seemed okay. That positive feeling diminished a couple of weeks later, however, when it became apparent that the horse was definitely not all right. John was giving a clinic and had Zip trotting around loose in the round pen. He and Josh noticed that the stallion was behaving strangely. Instead of displaying his willing, easygoing nature, they noticed that Zip was skittish to various sounds and became reluctant to participate. John grabbed a halter, took him out of the pen, and looked him all over. From his behavior, John had a sinking feeling that Zip's eyesight might be compromised.

Zip continued to behave skittishly, and it was determined that his sight was at the root. John searched vainly for a cure over the next several months, carting Zip around to various equine universities and vet hospitals. He took Zip to Tufts University, in New York, to have one of the nation's top equine eye specialists examine him. John watched as the veterinarian deployed the latest state-of-the-art diagnostic equipment to examine Zip and put the horse through a battery of tests.

John waited expectantly throughout all the procedures, hoping for good news on when Zip's eyesight would begin to return. When the doctor finally got all of the test results, he took John aside.

"John, Zip has a detached retina in his right eye, and the left is partially detached. I'm afraid that the condition is permanent." He prescribed a drug that would possibly help slow the deterioration. John dutifully administered the medication and slowly began to see results. He was elated. Zip's eyesight was returning! This prognosis was short-lived, however. Within a few months, Zip's sight for a second time became shadowy and eventually diminished completely.

Again, John made the rounds to the veterinary colleges. The doctor at Tufts told him, "I'm sorry, John. There's no therapy or operation that can be performed to restore his sight. But I do want you to know something. When an animal goes blind or has another major catastrophe, it's not the same as it happening to a person. If a person goes blind or becomes crippled, he will have a period of time where he says, 'how can this have happened to me? I don't deserve this—I'm a good

all of his own needs. That's why there are more horses on earth now than there ever have been. They are adaptable—to a harsh environment, to being domesticated, to various athletic careers. In comparison, the zebra is from the same family as the horse but has a much harder time adapting to a domestic life. Consequently, the zebra's numbers are dwindling due to many factors, one of which is that they must live a certain way and have more trouble adapting than horses. The horse is adaptable, which proves that he is not stubborn at all.

person.' He feels sorry for himself. He goes through a depression, then he goes through the motions of physical recovery, and physical therapy, but the real recovery doesn't start until he accepts what happened to him and he stops feeling sorry for himself. His recovery is going to be limited by how long he remains depressed, since people lose the acuity of their senses.

"I want you to know that Zip did not do that. He never felt sorry for himself, even for a day. He probably believes that all nineteen-year-old horses go blind, and that this is merely a normal part of his life."

John believed that God used that tragedy in his life to help him in other areas. It was a heartrending situation, but it taught him that when one door closes, another one opens. John told Susie, "You know, I think Zip can be an ambassador in many ways. He will show people that horses are still useful, even when they may not be able to see or may have some disability. We should never think about throwing them away just because of one limitation—as long as the horse is happy living life."

John believes that the Lord created the horse to be an athlete. When talking about his own blind horse, John said, "I can take Zip and spin him blazingly fast like a reining horse ten times in each direction—then lope him off and do flying lead changes. And Zip is actually just an average horse as far as athletic ability goes. Can you imagine closing your eyes, having someone spin you around, as fast as they could, and then say "now run a straight line"? Think of the physical coordination that it takes for a horse to do that. Ever see a blind person run at full speed? I can take Zip and still have him gallop flat out, which not only takes athletic ability but the courage to be able to keep balanced at a run."

Not everyone embraced John's spirituality. There were people from time to time who were turned off by the Jesus message, by the fish-and-Scripture reference that appears on all of his ads, by the time spent in his symposiums witnessing to the audience, by always keeping Christ in the forefront of his life. In 1998, at Equitana U.S.A., in Louisville, Kentucky, John was one of the featured guests in Freedom Hall. As usual, the place was packed. John ended his presentation by asking the audience how many of them had accepted Christ into their lives and a resounding number of hands and cheers went up. However, a small contingency hissed, "I hate when he does this. I wanted to see him work with horses, not attend a church service."

In John's Words

God gave humankind dominion over the horse. He told us to control him and guide him. It would be the same as my daughter Tammy Jo leaving her child with a baby-sitter. She didn't give little Tanner away to the baby-sitter, but she did entrust her to watch over him, care for him, and make him do his chores. She didn't give the baby-sitter the right to abuse him, beat him, or treat him badly. Part of caring for another means teaching the child to do things that are safe. It means taking responsibility for the child's safety and for what goes on around that child. So, like the baby-sitter, even though God gave man dominion over the animals, he gave us the responsibility as well. He didn't say that we could abuse the horse. God doesn't think that the horse is more important than we are, but He does want us to be accountable for what we do. We have to teach the horse, correct him, and keep him safe, just as we would a little child.

In John's Words

You see, people assume that because my son and daughter are MY children, they should naturally know what to do with any horse any time—and I worry because they didn't know everything that I knew, haven't been through everything that I have been through. People test them, or put them on horses that are dangerous. It's unfair to my family because God's taken such good care of me. I deserved to get hurt, yet I didn't. That's the advantage and disadvantage of being John Lyons's son or daughter. It is very risky for them, due to the reputation they feel the need to live up to. A lot of people will test them, and I guess I've always been concerned about that.

John knew that he could not reach everybody. "Some people do get turned off. I don't want to be offensive or push people away with my Christian walk. It's all in how I present it, I suppose. It's got to be somewhat balanced and in the right context, but also it's important that my audience knows where my training principles come from and why. If people understand the principles, they are more apt to obtain the same results."

John never makes it a requirement for people to attend his Sunday cowboy church service before starting the second day of the symposiums, but at the same time, he truly believes that there are some things that are more important than others. While his clinics are focused on training the horse in a way that is endearing and humane, John thinks that if he can affect and change people's lives, if he can open that door, begin the thought process, and let God do the rest—that is the reason he was put on earth.

And horse training has not been an easy life. Over the last two decades, John has worked with thousands of horses. He's had horses kick him, bite him, and roll over the top of him. He had one horse land a kick in the stomach with both back feet—powerful enough to kill a normal person—but John got up and went right back to work. John has never missed a day, nor has he ever been late for a clinic in twenty-one years.

At a clinic in San Diego, he broke his shoulder coming off a horse. Wincing in pain, John climbed back on and continued with the rest of the clinic for the next three hours. After it was over, he went to the hospital, got the shoulder taped up and immobilized, and was back working the next day. At a different clinic in Texas, John was violently bucked off three of the first four horses he worked with—and they were saddle broke. One wouldn't even let him get his foot in the stirrup.

John has never claimed that he is tougher than anyone else, more coordinated, more athletic, or even just plain luckier. Instead, Susie teasingly had the answer. "Everyone has a guardian angel," she says, laughing. "But you must have two, and I bet they're both standing in front of God with manure all over their wings, covered with sweat and dust, just begging for a reassignment."

One of the most difficult things that John has had to deal with is his own children's perception of his life with horses. His children grew up on the ranch and had horses from a very early age; they were in the saddle before they could walk, and they have traveled all over the nation with

John using Zip *after the horse went blind.*

him. All of them, at one time or another, joined the family business in different areas. But they don't know all that John really went through with the horses—some of the real setbacks and dangerous times, some of the bitter triumphs and the tiny breakthroughs.

The kids have seen John succeed and the business grow, along with his popularity and financial success. They know John was gone a great deal and worked really hard. But he is concerned that his kids got the wrong impression about making a living with horses. John believes the kids think, "Well, it can't be so bad since Dad does it. He deals with people, and his people can't be as hard as the ones I deal with, and I'm doing the same thing he's doing." But John is concerned that his kids will get injured trying to emulate him.

Chapter 10

LIFE OUTSIDE THE ARENA

The horse industry was changing rapidly and John

was instrumental in beginning many of those changes. He was one of the first trainers to advertise in national magazines such as *Horse Illustrated*, *Horse & Rider*, *Western Horseman*, and *Equus*. He was quite possibly the first trainer to include scriptures in those ads. It was important to him to include those scriptures because he felt that God had brought him to this point in his life and he wanted to give something back to Him. John was one of the first horsemen to bring one style of training to the industry; to get people to follow a single concept.

It was during this time that John went from being just a horse trainer, to a well-respected clinician and featured keynote speaker. In the mid 1990s, his popularity increased with the advent of horse expos, enormous trade shows with special guest celebrities, events, exhibitions, and seminars. John was in demand. He was the biggest draw at events such as Equitana in Kentucky, Equine Affaire in Ohio and Massachusetts, and other expositions. As his exposure grew, so did the demands of the people who wanted to see him and learn from him. John had gone from a cattle rancher to a horse trainer to a friend of everyone who owned a horse. After twenty years, he became America's most well-known and well-respected horse trainer.

During the late 1990s John continued to do the symposiums but by the end of 1999, he tried to cut back on the number quite a bit. The expos were growing and did not take as much time as the symposiums. By this time John had produced many videos and books and had developed a monthly newsletter, which was subscribed to by over 100,000 horse owners. In late 1999, he bought a plane so that he could fly out and come back home in the same weekend. The demands on John's time grew more and more. Susie traveled with John for a couple of years while Josh and Brandi were in high school. The kids were growing and soon all of them were out of high school. Once Josh graduated he began working full time with John giving clinics, symposiums, and teaching in the certification program. Tammy Jo got married and was on her own beginning a new life. Sandy graduated from college, got married, and started a family of her own.

As with most marriages there were hard times, and with all the work and time away from one another John and Susie began to grow apart. They faced the same everyday hardships that we all sometimes face and for reasons that had accumulated over their years together they felt their marriage could no longer go on.

In the fall of 2000, John and Susie's marriage had reached an end. What made their divorce more complicated than usual was that John had always shared his family life with the horse owners around the world. His family was a great part of his business because he always talked about them and shared stories of them when he was training; it seemed he shared his family with everyone. As any divorce is hard on a family, it would be no different for John and Susie and their children.

John and his family have done the best they can to move on and find new ground. It seems that now, both John and Susie are happier and the worst is over. Susie moved to Las Vegas and remarried in July of 2002, to Philip Patinier.

John is still dedicated to helping others with their horses and continues to work hard. He says, God knows that what we want most in our lives is peace, peace with others and peace with ourselves. Along the way, John met Jody Davini who has helped to bring a great deal of peace to his life. Together, John says, they find that happiness we all look for and sometimes never find.

Jody and John were married on June 7th, 2003. Jody has three kids who she and John adore, Jana, Mike, and Katie. John and Jody enjoy traveling together, whether it be on a vacation or to one of the horse

In Susie's Words

I live in Las Vegas and am active in my non-denominational Christian church, Canyon Ridge. I enjoy my home and pets, lead divorce recovery support groups, and still ride my horse BJ, as often as possible. I have a full life and visit my four kids and ten grandchildren often. My children all married wonderful spouses and I'm lucky to have a good relationship with each of them. I have a wonderful family and great friends all over the country. God has blessed me abundantly with love and happiness, and although there have been some sad moments, overall I wouldn't change anything. I feel quite fortunate to have found such a wonderful Christian man in Philip, and feel certain that God brought us together when He did. I look forward to whatever God has in store for Philip and I in the future.

shows. When they're not traveling, they like to play on the snowmobiles, take the motorcycle out for a ride, spend time in the mountains, and play with their horses.

While John now makes more time to have fun, he still enjoys training and traveling, helping horses and people. One of the advantages of his job is that he and Jody get the opportunity to meet some of the most fascinating people in the world. Along with the numerous awards he has received, John has also flown with the Blue Angels, been on jet skis in Australia, spent time diving for lobster in the Bahamas, wrestled alligators in Florida, flown helicopters, rode in a Nascar race car on race day at 200mph, and has met some of the best people in the world—horse owners.

Zip is still by his side and doing well. He gets to play mostly with the kids now, but also does regular exercise on a type of horse treadmill. Zip bred a mare for probably the last time in 2000, and the new baby is growing up and doing great on the ranch. She was even featured in a new foal training video.

The Cowboy Up Ranch is always improving, as John and Jody enjoy creating new projects. One of the things John loves most is playing on his tractors. He says the monotone of the diesel actually helps him to relax and sort out his thoughts. He and Jody both exercise every morning, and of course, there is always another show to go to. John's office continues to be extremely busy, and the future looks as bright as ever.

While John is still as busy as he wants to be, he diligently works right along side Josh, and they have become quite a team together. Josh has continued to do expos, clinics, and symposiums and has been teaching the certified trainers program on his own. John believes that Josh is one of the top five horse trainers in the world. John remains proud of all of his children as they have grown into responsible adults, good spouses, and excellent parents. He is happy that they all have a close relationship with Jesus Christ our Lord and only Savior.

And John's journey? Well, it's far from over—his star continues to shine, and his ways with horses continue to grow to legendary proportions. Time will tell how history writes the final chapter to this most trusted horseman.

In John's Words

We (John and Jody, pictured at left at the Cowboy Up Ranch) enjoy so much together and I could not love her more. She has added a great deal of happiness to my life.

A NOTE OF THANKS

I would like to take this moment to thank each

and every fan and friend out there for reading this book. Without you, my father, and my family, would not have accomplished what they have today. Your faith, your kindness, your gifts have been so magnificent and heartfelt. The dedication (and sometimes tireless work) from so many people across the nation is what has made this business successful, and we hope it has inspired everyone to become better horsemen and women.

As you can see, it wasn't all smoke and mirrors or a complete fairy tale like so many seem to think it was. Our lives, like many of yours, have been filled with trauma right along with the triumph. It wasn't much fun for several years, but during those years we had some great moments! Through it all, with God's help, we have persevered and we will continue to do so, like I know many of you will as well. My family thanks you from the deepest part of our hearts for opening your hearts to us.

I have met several people in this industry who have touched my heart and become beautiful, treasured friends. So many, in fact, that there are absolutely too many to name. However, there are a few whom I would like to thank personally for being there and inspiring me. Patty Colbert, thank you for your strength, your beauty, and your grace under pressure. I look up to you and admire you so much! Ken Banks, thanks for being such an inspiration to my father and myself, as well as a friend. Patty Russell, without you I would not know what real courage is. I am

always here for you. Pat Eskew, thanks for being a friend always, and for your continued loyalty to my family. Thanks to Linda Wingstrom, Judy Lemon, and Martha Saunders for being there for my family in so many ways that words cannot describe the love, faith, and devotion that is in your hearts. And to the rest of the JLS office staff, thank you for your hard work and patience. I know it often times goes unsaid, but Dad appreciates all that you do!

To Jody, thank you for putting up with all of us. I know at times it is extremely difficult, and I think your strength and compassion is downright inspirational. Thanks for always being that shoulder to lean on. You are loved.

Especially thanks to my sister, Sandy, without whom I would not be as strong as I am today. You are an inspiration, especially when it comes to sports, and I know you will always succeed in life, no matter what it is

that you do. Thanks for teaching me how to be such a good mom and for being the bestest friend a sister could ever have.

Thank you Josh, for being such a good listener—you are great at giving advice! You are absolutely awesome at everything you do. I am so proud of you and pray for your continued success into the future.

And to my mom, thanks for putting up with me. I know how bull-headed and stubborn I can be. You've always loved me, no matter what, and that support has gotten me through many rough times. Thanks for teaching me what loyalty is all about.

To my Dad, I love you always. You shine, as you always did, and I will forever respect and love you. You amaze me constantly. How you can continue to work so hard is beyond me. I will always be proud of what you have achieved in this lifetime. Thank you for passing on your wisdom, and your gift of using analogies to get your point across. You've taught me to never be afraid to ask questions, and now I never will.

To my loving and wonderful husband, my best friend, my soul mate, my cowboy, thanks for showing me what real love is. Thanks for understanding the complex woman that I am and for putting up with me. I'm sure it's difficult at times, but you do one heck of a job at it! I love you, Jason, with all that I am, and I always will.

To my beautiful and perfect son, Tanner, thank you for being the best boy in the whole wide world. You are always opening my eyes to new and wonderful things. You mean the world to me. I love you with all my heart and always will! I pray that I make you as proud of me one day, as I am of you.

And to our Father in Heaven, I know You've been there the whole time. *I thank You most of all* for sending your Son so that we could be saved. Thank you for being there every minute, even when I looked the other way. I have seen the miracles that You can create, and the gifts we sometimes take for granted. I love You for them with all my heart. Thank you, Lord, for all Your blessings, and all the beautiful angels down here on earth that inspire us to get through the rough stuff. Please continue to help me do Your Will.

May God be with you, your families, and your horses.

In Christ's Eternal Love,

Tammy Jo